# The Ultimate Handbook for TikTok Advertising

*Reach 1 Billion Individuals Quickly with These 10 Minutes Techniques*

# Table of Contents

Chapter One: How 80/20 Works & Why

Chapter Two: The Power Triangle

Chapter Three: 80/20 Conversion For TikTok Ads

Chapter Four: Digital Plumbing

Chapter Five: 80/20 Economics For TikTok Ads

Chapter Six: Generating Your Content

Chapter Seven: Targeting

Chapter Eight: Amplification

Chapter Nine: 80/20 Traffic Using TikTok Ads

Chapter Ten: Making Your TikTok Campaigns Fly

Chapter Eleven: 80/20 Scaling-up Massively

Chapter Twelve: WARNING: Ignore This Chapter at Your Extreme Peril

Chapter Thirteen: Finally Achieving Success With TikTok Ads

# Why This Is The Most Important Business Book You'll Read This Year

This graphic says it all:

| 2020 INTERNET TRAFFIC | VS. | 2021 INTERNET TRAFFIC |
|---|---|---|
| Google.com | 1 | TikTok.com |
| Facebook.com | 2 | Google.com |
| Microsoft.com | 3 | Facebook.com |
| Apple.com | 4 | Microsoft.com |
| Netflix.com | 5 | Apple.com |
| Amazon.com | 6 | Amazon.com |
| TikTok.com | 7 | Netflix.com |
| YouTube.com | 8 | YouTube.com |
| Instagram.com | 9 | Twitter.com |
| Twitter.com | 10 | WhatsApp.com |

*Image 1.1: 2021's Internet Traffic Rankings (Data - CloudFlare)*

TikTok's leap from #7 to #1 is astounding. (Jumping from #7 to #3 would be impressive!) Yet while most people will frame this as a business success story, or a "power of social media" story, or a "some folks didn't have anything better to do during a pandemic than binge-watching 30-second cat videos" story… the <u>real</u> story is:

*YOU will possess an incomparable advantage when you're among the first to master a new advertising medium.*

As the author of the world's most popular books on Google and Facebook ads, I have lived this not once but twice - not only for myself but for some 500,000 small businesses that have directly benefited from my books and courses.

I have consulted in over 300 industries and worked personally with thousands of entrepreneurs. *The surest way to gain a toehold, then foothold, then stranglehold in ANY market is having a NEW advertising medium create a NEW market.*

The hardest way to get ANY business off the ground is to saunter into an existing market and pit yourself against existing players who were already dominating existing media before you came in.

If you own a microbrew, what are your chances of getting traction on network television… against Coors and Budweiser? What are your odds of getting new customers in Super Bowl commercials?

Your odds are not merely small. Your odds are *zero*.

What are your odds on TikTok? On TikTok, you have a fighting chance. In fact, you have an advantage over big players because TikTok's users are likely to be much more interested in microbrews than the "King of Beers."

Between 2002 and 2007, Google Ads was the hottest new medium. Back then, the average guy on the street didn't even realize Google had ads in the first place.

Google opened its advertising system for business in February 2002 and I opened my first account two months later. The foothold I gained in those early days gave me a sustainable advantage for *years*. Exposure on Google was much less expensive and more effective than most other places you could advertise; I and thousands of others figured out how to "work the system" and once we were established, it was remarkably difficult for rivals to displace us.

Facebook hit the mainstream around 2011. The magic carpet ride began anew - with different rules.

For the first two years or so, Facebook ads were a dodgy wild west, working far better for some than for others. Slowly Facebook got their act together… Then once again for 4-5 years, Facebook traffic was cheap and plentiful *for people who knew how to work the system.*

Today, hundreds of thousands of companies owe their very existence to these platforms *because of their commitment to adapt their advertising, their marketing, their messaging, and their business models to the idiosyncrasies of their systems.*

You can predict with absolute certainty what will happen in the next 3-5 years with TikTok:

• Right now, in 2022, TikTok is very "wild west" as the world has not yet figured it out. It's unfamiliar to most advertisers, and legions of people only think of it as "free social media." Recall that it took a few years for the world to even figure out what you're supposed to do with social media platforms like Twitter. Today, it's entirely clear what you do with them. The same will happen with TikTok.

• During this wild west period, it will *seem* difficult, but most people will find that with persistent and consistent effort, it only takes a few weeks to get the hang of it.

• You will gain a lead over competitors, and while they are still content to wrangle with Facebook, Instagram, or YouTube, the secrets of TikTok begin to reveal themselves to you. As you participate with other members of our community, you'll experience esprit de corps as you discover things that literally *nobody else in the world* knows.

• You'll develop an almost preternatural sense of how the platforms work *and what your audiences respond to.*

• Your business will grow supremely adapted to TikTok and its idiosyncrasies and you'll grow to love the platform. Over time you'll accumulate an audience and fan base - *yes, even as an advertiser* and not an "organic" player - your position will solidify and you'll become an established player.

● During the next several years you will co-evolve with the platform. As you are able to invest more and more profits back into the business, it will become nearly impossible for rivals to compete with you.

## "But I don't even *like* TikTok"

Some people adore TikTok and spend all day there. Other people wish it would go away. Same with Facebook and Google and everybody else. All of us have feelings about the various platforms.

*"TikTok is an emotional firehose."*

*"TikTok is too irrational."*

*"It's so politically correct."*

*"It's just singing, dancing, silly stuff, and entertainment."*

*"I see videos then I never find them again."*

*"People randomly hate stuff for no reason."*

Guess what… I don't "like" Facebook. I don't enjoy spending time there and I log in to look at my news feed maybe once a month. But that hasn't kept me from giving Facebook lots of money and getting *lots* of clients from them.

You don't have to like the New York Times - or even be a reader - to advertise in the New York Times. The question is simple: Will the platform give you more customers? If the answer is yes, spend the money and pick up new clients.

## "But the only people on TikTok are kids and 20-somethings."

Not true. My wife is 52 and she's a TikTok fanatic. For Halloween, she dressed up as her favorite TikTokker, "V" of Under The Desk News. Don't forget - people were saying the exact thing about Facebook 10 years ago.

Fact is, people of *all* ages are on TikTok. If you're selling industrial presses to 55-year-old men, TikTok is probably not your best source of traffic - but yes, millions of 55-year-old men are on TikTok. Please remember that everyone has a different feed that is immediately and eerily customized by the world's most addictive algorithm. The older half of the population will be the fastest-growing segment of new TikTok users for the next few years.

You'll recall that the "only 20-somethings" argument was true when Facebook first came out too.

Here's what's important to understand: we're not teaching you to "go viral." We're not teen influencers trying to become social media stars. What we can do is drive great business results without *needing* to go viral, just like we do with Facebook and Google ads. We don't need to act like celebrities!

40+ is the fastest-growing segment. And we are already seeing the singing and dancing giving way to more educational videos. Ironically, it's less about TikTok becoming more like Facebook, but Facebook needing to become like TikTok. In the latest earnings call, Zuckerberg noted that Reels would have to compete.

Facebook (now Meta) conducted a nine-day diary study on teens and adults in the US on their session-level experiences using TikTok and Instagram Reels.

This extract from the summary highlights this point:

"Most participants preferred TikTok compared to Reels at the end of the study, even if they started out as Reels users."[1]

## "Is TikTok good or bad?"

I do not believe it is a good thing that a billion people are spending this much time on TikTok or Facebook or Instagram. I didn't think it was a good thing when the same number of people were watching TV for five hours a day, either.

But nobody asked me. And they didn't ask you. That's just what people do.

If you're going to be successful as a marketer or entrepreneur, you must live in the "is" world—not the "should be" world. In the "is" world, 95 percent of people float around in a miasma of mild hypnosis, looking forward to their next hit of "like" and "share" happy juice, or to extract their "pound of flesh" out of some stranger who disagrees with them about politics.

This book is all about how you get inside the minds of TikTok users and get them to do what you want them to do. Whether you're doing business as a church, a school, a winery, a life coach, a car manufacturer, or a seller of aluminum siding, you've got a job to do.

There is a difference between using TikTok as a business to fulfill business objectives and using it as a consumer for entertainment. As business owners, we need to go where people congregate en masse, and right now, TikTok is the place to be.

People are going to spend their time and money somewhere. If they spend their time and money with you, you succeed. If they spend it with someone else, you fail. The fact that people are in a state of partial hypnosis provides a platform where you can sell them your product or service.

In this book, you'll learn how to harness that power.

## The "Free Model" vs. "Make $1 Model"

The rise of YouTube Celebs (especially with them getting a share of ad revenue) has created a hysteria around social media influencers that have inspired thousands of aspiring stars and starlets to try as hard as humanly possible to "go viral."

They desire to become the next Gary Vaynerchuk / Hank Green / Laura Izumikawa / Joe Rogan / Addison Rae / Jordan Peterson / Tess Holiday / Vsauce / Vitus "V" Spehar / Emma Chamberlain / Abigail Behar / Humans Of New York. They post, comment, like, tweet, blog, V-blog 24/7 hoping that the algorithmic gods will smile upon them.

They record videos everywhere they walk and drive. They opine about everything under the sun, hoping that just one of those videos will get a million views.

This method works for a vanishingly small number of the people who try it. I believe it requires a certain indefinable "magic" or "star power" to work. I do not think it is at all honest to advertise this as a system that works reliably for anybody and everybody.

The greatest deception of the Free Model is the notion that it's "free." It's only free if you consider weeks, months, and years of your blood, sweat, and life (and your absence from the lives of your friends and family members) to be "free."

Oh yeah… and just because they're internet famous doesn't guarantee they're rolling in dough. Very few internet celebs are actually "rich."

There is another method that is much more reliable, often overlooked, and far more formulaic and predictable. I call it the "Make $1 Model." It's where 80% of the wealth resides. And it's far more consistent and reliable than the free model.

The Make $1 Model says:

Test…

- Ads
- Landing Pages
- Offers

With **small** advertising dollars and **small** quantities of time until you **make one dollar**.

What does "make one dollar" mean?

It means:

Spend $10 and make $11.

Spend $100 and make $101.

Spend $1000 and make $1001.

In other words, *just run the machine and tinker with it until it's in the black.* You don't worry about your labor. You can fix that later… for now you just need to generate media exposure without losing money. Once you solve that problem the rest is pretty straightforward. The hard part is over and you can scale up.

How do you run the machine?

You test ads until you get a good Click Thru Rate.

You test videos until you get a high completion rate.

You test landing pages until you get a good signup rate.

You test offers until you find one that sells well.

**This is incomparably easier than trying to become the next Joe Rogan.** And you can literally do this with lunch money if you don't have a lot of cash. **Most entrepreneurs that I know - thousands of people who make six and seven-figure incomes, and many companies that have been sold for millions and tens of millions of dollars - built their businesses THIS way.**

Software companies, manufacturing firms, subscription services, consultants and coaches, dentists and cosmetic surgeons, delivery services, real estate investors, sellers of nutritional supplements, and household goods.

"Make $1" is the 21$^{st}$-century version of what Claude Hopkins was teaching in his classic book "Scientific Advertising" written in 1918. This is eminently reliable.

It's almost inevitable that by the time you've tested 30 ads, 10 landing pages, and 5 offers that you'll have a sales machine that nets you a positive return.

This book shows you how to do that.

## How much should you spend to acquire a customer?

There's a really simple way to answer this question, which is great for beginners… then, once you have your sea legs, the answer changes a bit.

The simple answer is: If you can invest $100 in advertising and product costs and sell your product for $101 and literally "make one dollar," then you are over the hump.

If you're new, then hang on to this and run with it until you make one dollar.

If you can acquire a customer at break-even or better, then as soon as you sell them anything else, you're profitable. This invokes…

## The Magic Gumball Machine Question:

*If you had a magic gumball machine, so that when you put money in, out comes a new customer, what's the most you'd be willing to put in?*

This is an incredibly powerful question. First, most people don't know the answer. Second, it reduces customer acquisition to dollars and cents, which is the goal of all advertising. Third, it naturally invites you to consider the Lifetime Value of a customer, instead of only the first sale.

For a brand new advertising medium with cheap click prices, early in the game advertisers will be able to make a profit acquiring a new customer the very first time. But that doesn't last very long. Soon the world figures it out and prices go up.

So again, for beginning advertisers, your goal is to "make one dollar."

For more advanced advertisers, the real question is: How far negative are you willing to go to acquire your customer? If your margin on a product is $30, can you afford to spend $35? $40? 50?

The thing that makes you able to "go deep" is your ability to generate repeat sales. If your first sale is $50 and you're able to spend $100 to acquire that $50 customer, because you know that in 3-6 months you'll get all that money back and more, you become a formidable player in the ad marketplace.

I've got a story for ya...

A few weeks ago there was a knock on the door. My 11-year-old daughter answered. It was the dad of two of her friends. They lived across the street from our house for several years. She still sees them from time to time.

The dad asked for me but I wasn't available. The next day he texted.

"I've got a good friend who follows your work. She runs a nonprofit. Could we stop by and ask you a few questions?"

Since our kids are friends, I said yes. Turns out his friend performs a very particular kind of therapy. She gets exceptional results for her clients. She began peppering me with questions, which were all over the place and vibed mostly with the "Free Model."

After digging for a while, I discovered that she had at one time successfully sold an expensive "48-hour immersion experience" where clients make great progress in a very short period of time.

I told her:

*Just sell THAT. Do not pass go, do not collect $200, do not blink or even think until you have figured out how to run an ad, build a list and sell seats to your workshop. Don't worry about whether you make a profit on the first workshop. Just make ONE dollar.*

A week later she sent a thank you note solemnly pledging to do precisely that.

Thus her journey began.

# Setting The Stage

My trusted friend Ken McCarthy recommended Richard Koch's landmark book *The 80/20 Principle*.

By the time I got to page 14, my mind was on fire. I saw an entirely new and different dimension: 80/20 APPLIES TO EVERYTHING. A thousand new connections formed, connections I'd never made until that very instant.

Koch's book, which I had just begun to read, would prove to be the most pivotal business book I'd ever picked up.

And that's exactly how my book, *80/20 Sales & Marketing* has been received by others. Since the first edition was published back in 2013, I have received thousands of emails from entrepreneurs with their own a-ha moments.

They quote parts of the book back to me that made the biggest impact, changing many lives for the better.

It's because of my own a-ha's with Koch's 80/20 book that this book you're reading now exists.

And just like my original book on 80/20, this book focuses on the 80/20 principle and incorporates my "Pareto Points" so that you can apply 80/20 to the reading of this book too.

Before I introduce you to my co-author and TikTok Advertising, here's a quick run-down on how the "Pareto Points" work.

### Pareto Points

You can read 20 percent of this book and get 80 percent of the benefit when you read the special sections called "Pareto Points," which are indicated with the logo that looks like this.

As you read the book, look out for this icon because it means the material is *extremely* important. If you simply read those points and nothing else, you'll have applied the 80/20 principle.

Now, the very first thing you have to do is get real with yourself and realize that for you, playing around on social media is NOT the same as RUNNING social media or CONTROLLING social media—pulling the puppet strings of the world.

Millions of people quit their jobs to start a business. They're essentially being supported by their spouses. They go to work every day, and while they are changing bedpans at the hospital, they think their spouse is working when, in fact, they are just goofing off on Facebook/Instagram/TikTok all day. Doing stuff that sort of kind of *looks* like work.

And making zero money.

That person is like the chef who, instead of cooking, just stands in the kitchen and shovels food in their mouth all day.

Well, this is a book about making money on TikTok—not screwing around on TikTok. TikTok Ads is a serious endeavor. You will get nowhere with those bad habits. You either pull the strings of the Matrix from outside the Matrix, or you're in the Matrix being entertained by it. You can't do both.

I never log into TikTok as a standard user until after 5:30 p.m. Most days I don't log in at all. But on the very same day, we may spend hours in the TikTok Interface being the chef and pulling the strings of the Matrix.

**Never confuse activity with productivity**. The two are not the same.

As a TikTok Advertiser, you are tasked with injecting creativity into the system, then measuring and tracking the results. You use your tracking tools—not checking out TikTok notifications every two seconds. Pay careful attention to what works and what doesn't. Notice trends, not stuff. Accept your job, which is to influence the hypnotized masses who are coming to TikTok for their entertainment addiction.

You are not the person who comes to the restaurant and feeds their face for five hours. You work in a restaurant. You serve up great dishes. You only sample enough of the soup to know whether it tastes good or bad; then you go on and create more great cuisine.

Sorry if this sounds preachy. But I have many customers and clients whose productivity, sales, profits, and income absolutely skyrocketed after they:

- deleted social media apps from their phone (yes, *deleted*)).

- realized that the world is in an incessant, never-ending conspiracy to rob you of time, attention, creativity, and mental space.

- closed the TikTok tab in their browser.

- entirely stopped using TikTok in the usual fashion during work hours.

- blocked all email notifications from TikTok and all other social media.

- halted ALL smartphone notifications from all social media apps—no banners on the screen, no little red numbers on your app icons, no distractions.

Go on. Do all of the above—now! If you don't, it will be devilishly difficult to master the key concepts in this book. Instead, TikTok will master you.

TikTok is set to take over the world in the next 3-5 years. It is the aquarium that lots of people want to swim in. TikTok is your portal to influencing the world—their behavior, their opinions, their purchases, their relationships. You need to pull the levers without letting TikTok addiction take control of you.

TikTok knows what its users look like, think, enjoy, and visit because it is the world's largest:

- **Short-form mobile video-sharing site.** During a recent test, Statista found that users watched 167 million videos every minute on TikTok.

- **Thought-sharing site.** Recently, Upfluence found micro-influencers average engagement rates on YouTube were 1.63%, but on TikTok, average engagement hovered around 17.96%.

- **Liking site.** TikTok is the most visited website on the internet, surpassing even Google. The average US TikTok user uses the app for more than an hour a day.

- **Linking site.** TikTok gives more variety (more trends, creators, and topics) to users in a session than competing sites, which helps contribute to increased sharing.

- **Demographic and psychographic gathering engine.** TikTok's algorithm tracks and stores users' IP addresses, messages, and the amount of time they view each video. They also track users' interactions with advertisers. All of this helps increase the effective targeting of ads.

Even with Google and Facebook's gargantuan lead, TikTok is becoming the world's most used app, especially as the internet continues its trajectory toward easy mobile device access and addiction to short-form mobile video.

Now that's enough from me. For this book, I've chosen to partner with a subject matter expert on TikTok Advertising and how you can apply it in your business with the 80/20 principle.

My co-author is Dennis Yu, host of the CoachYu Show. Dennis is not only a world-class expert in TikTok Advertising, he is one of the world's top ads and analytics experts. He built the internal analytics at Yahoo! before most of us had even started dabbling on the web. Across clients, his agencies have spent over a billion dollars in social advertising and expect to do the same on TikTok.

As we are co-authors of this book, you'll continue to hear from us both. You'll know when authors change as you'll see an image of Dennis or myself, indicating that the content following is the corresponding voice.

~ Perry Marshall

## Introduction to Dennis Yu

The first thing I want you to know, as we dive into the world of TikTok Ads, is that we're not professional TikTok influencers who are spending 6 hours per day on social media for a living, trying to go "viral."

**As professionals who have service-based and info-product businesses, we typically spend 30 minutes a week producing TikTok content for**

**our audience.**

**Yes. You read that right. 30 minutes.**

15-second raw cellphone selfie videos (no need to edit or get fancy) are all we need to make TikTok videos — quick tips, sharing knowledge, that sort of thing. Simple.

Here's the thing you need to understand... TikTok's algorithm is incredibly smart at figuring out who we are trying to reach — even in business to business and local service businesses.

Pareto
Point

So acquiring leads and customers requires only small audiences and low production, compared to "influencers" who need millions of views to earn ad dollars.

We are the advertisers spending $20 a day to grow our business by having TikTok be an extension of our existing funnel using existing assets (not new content for TikTok. We're all about repurposing what's already working).

Inside this book, we're going to share how you can do the same.

So let's dive in.

# Chapter One:
# How 80/20 Works & Why

A few years ago I held a seminar in Chicago titled "The 80/20 Seminar for Direct Marketing." To my knowledge, it was the first of its kind. It cost $3,000 to attend and I had about 80 people in the room. All of them ran one business or another, most of them online.

To illustrate the all-pervasive nature of 80/20, I said, "Everybody, stand up if you have shoes on."

Everyone stood. I said, "If you own fewer than 4 pairs of shoes, please sit down." A bunch of people sat down, and about 50 were still standing.

"If you own fewer than 8 pairs of shoes, sit down."

More people sat down, about 30 left.

"If you own fewer than 16 pairs of shoes, sit down."

Thirteen people, 9 of them women, still standing.

"32 pairs of shoes."

Three women standing.

I smiled. "Don't be embarrassed, ladies. Just tell the truth, cuz I'm illustrating a principle here. How many of you have more than 64 pairs of shoes?"

Two sit down. One left standing. She cringes with embarrassment.

"How many shoes do you have?"

"Umm, about 80."

"Thank you so much. You can sit down now. Give this woman a hand!"

Everyone clapped. "20 percent of the people own 80 percent of the shoes. Can you see that?" I said. All nodded in agreement.

*Almost everything is like that.*

Not absolutely everything—but most things. Shoes, domains, names, Bible verses, trips to Vegas, pearl necklaces, consumption of dinner napkins, tubes of lipstick. Rabbit populations, streams, rivers, size of cities in southern Argentina, and passengers on London's underground "Tube" trains. Net incomes, profit margins, software development timelines, foreclosures, trips to the tavern, and trips to the emergency room. Diameters of stars and planets, and the size of craters on the moon.

Why rattle off this scattered list of things in a business book about TikTok Ads? Because if you can see 80/20 at work in this list, you can identify it in any part of your business, including TikTok from a sales and marketing perspective.

Once you've learned to recognize it, you can't *not* see it. Look at the tree outside your window: 80 percent of the sap travels through 20 percent of the branches.

If you have 30 customers, you're tempted to treat them all the same. Well, they're really not the same at all. Odds are, 20 percent of your business comes from just one of them. The size of those customers really looks like this, in Image 1.2.

### How Most People Think about Their Customers

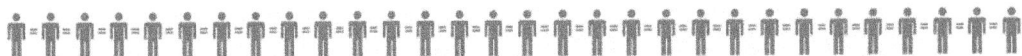

### The Truth about Your Customers

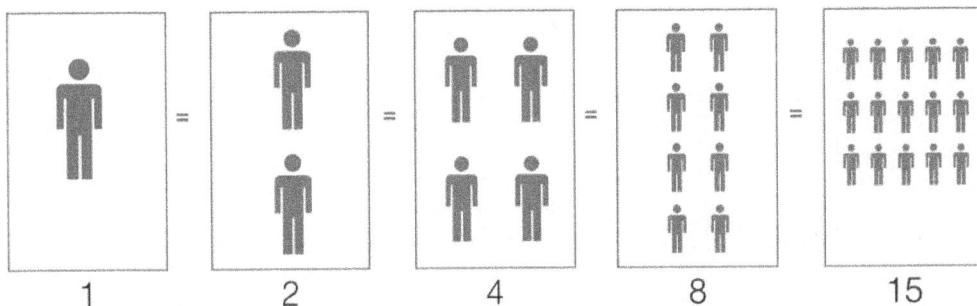

*Image 1.2: The Truth About Your Customers*

**All of these things obey the 80/20 principle.** That's because

**Pareto Point** 80/20 isn't a mere rule of thumb, and it's not just for business. It's a law of nature.

It's not the exact number 80/20 that's the rule; it's the principle of *positive feedback* (here, we're not talking about YOU somehow rewarding your customers with incentives. This is the *scientific principle* of positive feedback), which is when behavior is rewarded so that it produces more of the same behavior. Sometimes it's 60/40 or 70/30; sometimes it's 90/10 or 95/5. The exact numbers aren't so important. But it's always there.

And with some very simple tools that come as a bonus with this book, you can punch in a few numbers on your phone or computer in seconds and make spooky-accurate guesses for yourself. At lunch, on the back of a napkin, you'll be able to shuffle through all kinds of ordinary facts about your business—how many customers, how many VIP members, how many shoplifting incidents, the number of people who opened yesterday's email. You'll easily assign dollar figures to all and instantly know which opportunities are worth pursuing and which ones waste your time and money.

## 80/20 101
*80/20 says 80 percent of your results come from 20 percent of your efforts, and 20 percent of your results come from the other 80 percent.*

**Pareto Point** The *real* power in 80/20 is that you can disregard 80 percent of the roads in your city, only look at the top 20 percent, and the 80/20 rule will *still* apply. 80 percent of the 80 percent of traffic is on 20 percent of the 20 percent of roads.

That means 64 percent of the travelers drive on 4 percent of the roads. That's $80/20^2$.

Then we do it again: 80 percent of the 80 percent of the 80 percent of the traffic runs on 20 percent of the 20 percent of the 20 percent of the roads.

In other words, 52 percent of the travelers drive on 0.8 percent of the roads. That's $80/20^3$.

And it can keep going and going.

80/20 says that if you have 10 rooms in your house, you spend almost all your time in two or three of them. It says if you hire 10 salespeople, two will generate 80 percent of the sales and the other eight will generate only 20 percent of the sales.

That means that *person for person*, the two are SIXTEEN TIMES as effective as the eight. That's right—a good salesperson isn't 50 percent better, he or she is 16X better. That means there's huge leverage in 80/20: much to be gained if you pay attention, much to lose if you don't.

## The 80/20 of TikTok Ads

Now that you're up-to-speed on how 80/20 works, let's consider how it applies to TikTok Advertising and your business.

When we apply the 80/20 to TikTok Ads, we don't have to be like YouTubers and TikTok influencers, who abide by a regimen of 6-7 videos a day and one live video per day.

Instead, we focus on massive repurposing of what's already working on other platforms such as Facebook and YouTube, including reuse of content from your other platforms too — then we have to cut it down to 15-second videos (22-30 seconds is the outside limit of attention) if we haven't already.

We can reuse these short videos across TikTok, Instagram stories, and Snapchat — they are all "stories" driven by an algorithm that prioritizes watch time.

We can further 80/20 this as well because once we find winners (which is usually 1 in 10 videos), we can put them into an ad set where we boost it for $10 a day forever. It's likely that this daily ad spend will decrease over time - maybe down to $1 a day eventually.

Thus, the concept of our "greatest hits" (aka the 20 percent) is that as we find winners, we don't have pressure to keep making more, although we want to always keep improving (winners stay on).

By taking this approach, you can 80/20 your way to finding the best performing ads and then 80/20 things further to improve what's already working.

In this book, we're going to focus on identifying what's already working on your other platforms, like Facebook and YouTube, create short, 15 second videos for TikTok, and then zero in on those that are your "greatest hits" so that we can further optimize from there.

**Side Note:** Technically, the sweet spot for going viral on sharing information on TikTok is at 22 seconds.

Whereas on Instagram, a story has to be under 15 seconds.

And only the top TikTok creators have the panache and style to get people to watch to the end of a video (video completion rate is huge) — so 15 seconds is what we want to shoot for. That's your 80/20 right there.

---

## PARETO SUMMARY
---

▷ The real power of 80/20 is $80/20^2$, $80/20^3$, and so on. It keeps going until you run out of things to count.

▷ When we apply 80/20 to TikTok Ads, we don't have to be like YouTubers and TikTok influencers, who abide by a regimen of 6-7 videos and one live video per day.

▷ We focus on what's already working on other platforms when we start TikTok ads. Repurposing what's already working is key.

▷ We 80/20 our TikTok Ads and focus on the winners. We don't have pressure to keep making more, although we want to always keep improving (winners stay on).

# Chapter Two:
# The Power Triangle

Before we dive into all things TikTok Ads, it's important that you understand the three steps to selling anything.

1. Traffic - you need humans to sell to, without raising their defenses, if at all possible.

2. Conversion - you need to convince the person that what you have is going to solve their problem.

3. Economics - you have to give that person something that's valuable and get their money -- in other words, the exchange of value actually needs to WORK so that you can be profitable

These three steps form a **Power Triangle** that governs everything that happens in sales and marketing, no matter what channel you're focused on.

You should always be suspicious of complicated things. You should be even more suspicious of people who make simple things complicated.

The beautiful thing about the Power Triangle is how simple it is. Einstein knew he was onto something big with a simple equation:

$$e = mc^2$$

Even a seventh-grader can deal with that, with a little help from their science teacher.

Things that are *true* and *correct* tend to have that sort of simplicity.

This brings me to the Power Triangle, a brainchild of Jack Born. The Power Triangle, in Image 2.1, always takes you where you need to go, and the 80/20 in the center always focuses you on the points of highest effectiveness.

It's a work of genius.

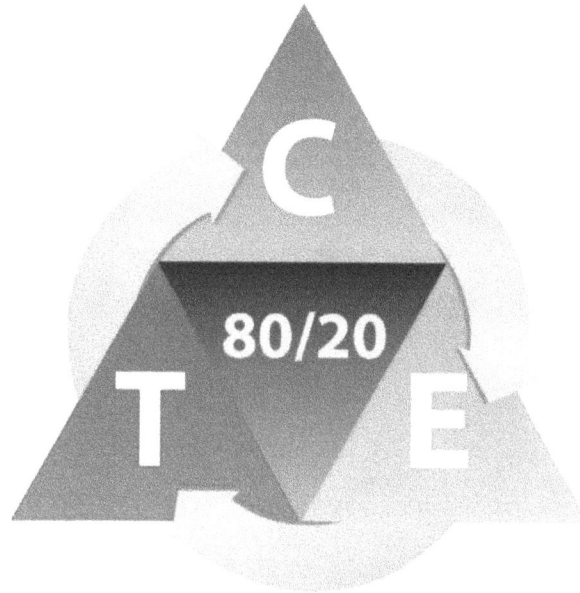

*Image 2.1: The Power Triangle and 80/20*
*(Illustration by Danielle Flanagan)*

**Pareto Point**

In order to sell something, you have to get Traffic; then you have to Convert the traffic. Economics means you have to make some money on what you sell. That's why you're in business.

When you make a profit you can reinvest it in getting more Traffic, Converting the traffic, and further improving your Economics. And so it goes, clockwise in a circle. It's a spiral of never-ending Traffic, Conversion, and Economics.

That's the essence of marketing. It describes every *human* transaction.

You can apply it to romance or volunteering for the Peace Corps or trading favors with your fishing buddies.

*Image 2.2: 80/20 is multi-layered*
*(Illustration by Danielle Flanagan)*

The first thing to notice about the Power Triangle is that the 80/20 principle sits in the center. It's there for a good reason.

80/20 is in the center because everything revolves around putting less in and getting more out. And finally, 80/20 is fractal. Inside every top 20 percent is another top 20 percent.

The second thing I want you to notice about the Triangle is: **You needed to go counterclockwise to decide how to sell something.**

This means the primary skill you must master in marketing is *thinking backward*...

Let's look at the Power Triangle and how it applies to TikTok ads.

## The Power Triangle and TikTok Ads

TikTok is about getting the (right) data in place, inserting the content, and putting money in the machine — which loosely aligns with the Power Triangle above.

We can assume that anyone who has a business has already found a compelling offer (economics) and market fit (which drives conversion).

Thus, TikTok is about replicating this content/offering x audience/target into every other channel.

Whoever your audience is, we can find them on every channel. For the same reason that your Facebook audiences are increasingly on TikTok, they are also on YouTube, Snapchat, and Twitter.

Remember, whatever content/offering is working, we want to reuse that in TikTok - to take what's already proven and get more out of it. Thus, instead of 80/20, it's more like 90/10.

It just so happens that **TikTok has the most powerful (addictive) algorithm to find and hook audiences.** Thus, the "traffic" component is largely around creating content in the right format (hook and "watch to the end"), which is then amplified by the ad dollars you invest.

Let's use an example.

Let's say your traffic is TikTok ads, your conversion is a website sales page, and your economics is that you offer marketing training for real estate agents.

Inside those 15-second TikTok videos we can find another Triangle, as shown in Image 2.3.

*Image 2.3: Traffic = People who see the ad;*
*Conversion = Ad copy;*

Let's say your visitors land on a page that offers free training in exchange for their email address, company name, and first name. There's a Triangle there too:

- Traffic = people who land on your page
- Conversion = people who opt in and the reasons they did.
- Economics = what they get in exchange for their email address and the value of that address to you

**Pareto Point** The *economic value* of an email address is huge. Even with all the channels that are available to get in front of potential customers, email is still the center of the marketing universe. **The number-one function of your website is to collect an email address** from your visitor before they leave.

Also - *very important* - email is one of the few communication channels that is not controlled by a big corporation. You cannot own a social media following, but you can own an email list. If you're a YouTuber and you have a million followers, and YouTube shuts your account down, it's game over… because on YouTube you don't own your followers. Same with Twitter, Facebook, TikTok, and Instagram. This might not seem like a big deal today, but across months and years, this is *massively* important.

You need to be collecting email addresses and maintaining a relationship with your audience via email. After all these years, a warm email audience still continues to be the easiest way to make the cash register ring.

The TikTok ad still has an 80/20 ratio: The first 5-7 seconds of your ad influence most of your response. Then the most influential element is the offer made in your ad.

While the first 1-2 seconds are what count as far as the social media networks go in how they define a video view (which is enough for brand recall), this length of time is not enough to convince or teach. This is why the first 5-7 seconds of your ad will garner the most of your results.

Now that we've explained the Power Triangle, let's break down the three steps and focus on how you can use TikTok Advertising to impact your traffic, conversion, and economics.

## *Using TikTok to Reach a New Audience*

The Paperless Agent is a real estate training company that specializes in teaching realtors how to bring their marketing into the digital age. They have various subscription groups and training products for sale, but the first step in their funnel is to offer free training resources covering a wide range of topics as lead magnets. They then use email remarketing to deliver follow-up content connected to the original lead source.

The Paperless Agent has had great success with these lead gens on Facebook, but is looking to expand their platforms and test the new audiences available on TikTok.

Our goal together was to generate leads using two of their top-performing lead magnets.

### Traffic–Content and Targeting:
For content, The Paperless Agent team created 3 short videos, one relating to both lead magnets and then one focused video for each topic.

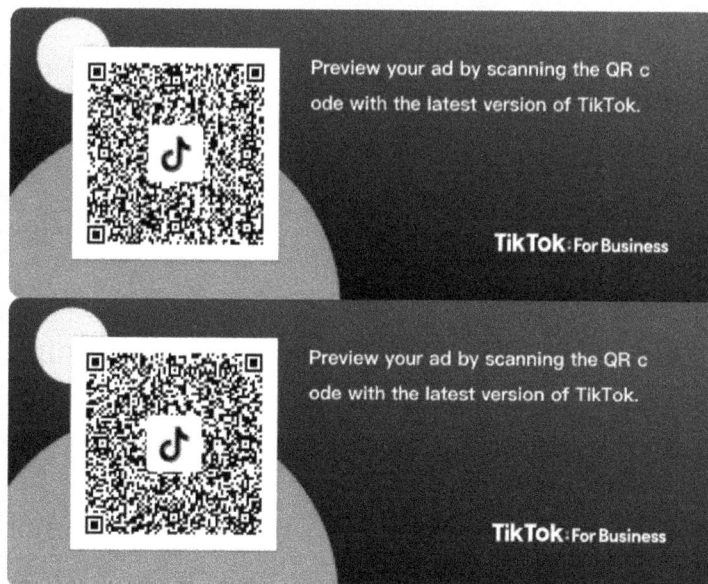

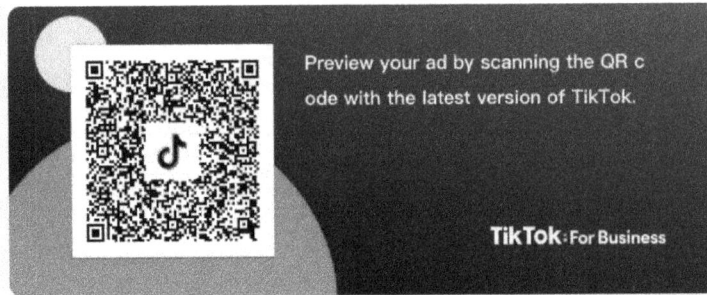

Note the natural movement and the attention-grabbing hook in each video. These videos are excellent examples of how to create compelling videos around a product.

Because this campaign was The Paperless Agent's first TikTok campaign, we did not have many options for remarketing audiences, so we elected to use the interest targeting options available on TikTok.

**Conversion–Campaign Metrics:**
- Spend: $296.56
- Impressions: 74,319
- CPM: $3.99
- 6 Second Video Views: 6,896
- Clicks: 321
- Downloads: 9
- CPA: $32.95

**Economics:**
Our campaign ran for around 3 weeks and we spent close to $300. This $300 generated 9 leads at a cost per lead of around $32.95.

These results are very promising, especially considering the interest-based nature of our targeting.

One thing to note is the very low CPM metric for the campaign. When you are bidding for conversions as we are here, you are competing in the most expensive auction on any given digital platform.

We've seen conversion stage CPMs rise on Facebook and other platforms consistently over the last few years. For a high ticket item like real estate training, the ability to generate impressions at a CPM of $3.99 in the conversion stage is incredible and shows that our content and targeting are resonating with each other.

**Key Takeaways:**
We had a few things reaffirmed to us through this campaign and found some other insights to share with you.

First, this case study demonstrates that the content principles we have shared with you work. Content drives your performance on all social platforms and this is especially true on TikTok.

Our second takeaway is that TikTok interest-based targeting may be worth testing for your business. Social platforms, in general, are moving away from strict targeting rules and this seems to hold true for Facebook. This doesn't eliminate the usefulness of remarketing audiences or other customer lists but allows you to start testing right away.

Finally, we learned how heavily TikTok favors new content. We would have loved to keep these ads running permanently with the results they were generating, but we saw that after 3 weeks the content just stopped delivering. Our payment method was still set-up and we had no errors there, but the ads just stopped delivering. We tested the same ads with a different audience and again saw little delivery.

**TikTok heavily favors recency in its algorithm, so in order for you to be successful, you need to be consistently creating and publishing content.**

Once you find a winner, you can and should take the topic and style into consideration, but you will still need to be creating new content for the platform.

## PARETO SUMMARY

▷ The Power Triangle always takes you where you need to go, and the 80/20 in the center always focuses you on the points of highest effectiveness. Traffic, conversion, and economics.

▷ Great marketers think backwards, which means starting with economics first.

▷ Your website's most important goal is to ensure an email address is collected before someone leaves it.

▷ A TikTok ad still has an 80/20 ratio: The first 5-7 seconds of your ad influence most of your response. Then the most influential element is the offer made in your ad. 80/20.

# Chapter Three:
# 80/20 Conversion For TikTok Ads

To optimize your TikTok ads, we'll focus on a few areas using the 80/20 approach.

But before we do that, let's revisit The Five Power Disqualifiers®.

Developed by my good friend, John Paul Mendocha, who reduced the sales process into five essential requirements that are *always* present when a sale is made. These go hand in hand with the Power Triangle because these five things define the *who* of the traffic that you're trying to buy.

This is a slimmed-down version.[2]

## The Five Power Disqualifiers®

1. Do they have money? As in, does the market you're selling to have money or not?
2. Do they have a bleeding neck? Aka a dire sense of urgency, a problem that needs to be solved right now.
3. Do they buy into your unique selling proposition?
4. Do they have the ability to say YES? I.e. are you getting in front of the right people?
5. Does what you sell fit in with their overall plans?

When applied, each one of these disqualifiers typically gets rid of the bottom 80 percent of whomever you're dealing with.

Keep this in mind as we go through the rest of this chapter.

## How Felipe Mate amplified TikTok ads to build an email list of thousands in a few months

Say you've got a great product but are camera shy. Or say there are a million other things that keep you from getting your phone out and making a 15-second TikTok video.

What do you do then?

Consider the story of Felipe Mate whose company, Stack Marketer, gained thousands of new subscribers in just a few months.

So far, Felipe estimates his total conversions at around 3,201 and his cost per acquisition at under two dollars.

Those are great numbers, but just as inspiring are some of the ways Felipe pushed through some of the barriers that could have kept him from his success.

Problem one? Felipe is not a native English speaker. Stack Marketer is a Portuguese company, and because they're trying to reach an American audience with their product, they had to figure out a way to bridge this language gap.

To amplify their message, Felipe's team enlisted 20 influencers to help them with their campaign. For around a total of 4,000 USD, Felipe had each of these influencers make a short organic video that compelled their audiences to subscribe to Stack Marketer.

For each video released, they had influencers put Stack Marketers URL at the end of the post.

This brought about a second challenge: how do you measure attribution with an organic post that doesn't allow for links?

As a rough guide, the Stack Marketer team measured the effectiveness of each post by watching for spikes in traffic when each of them went live. They also used other engagement signals like views, likes, and comments to get an idea of the success of each post.

The third challenge came when they finally started running ads on these posts. Initially, they found that they weren't getting the number of leads they expected. But this disappointment led to a better solution when they found TikTok leadgen forms. These built-in TikTok forms reduced friction and increased their signups.

The final challenge when running this campaign just took a little communication. Because his company was in Portugal, TikTok wouldn't allow them to advertise to the US. Felipe says he was in constant contact with his TikTok manager and was able to eventually get them to give him access to the US market.

Felipe found workarounds for reasons that could have held him back from putting his videos together and pushing forward. From our years of experience with Facebook ads, we know that one of the biggest problems businesses have with running ads on social media is just not running enough of them.

To amplify your message, you've got to keep making content and continue to push through anything that might hold you back.

## Learn Quickly and Iterate Constantly

*"I tried it and it didn't work"* is one of the most common things we hear from clients and wannabe marketers — one shot and they're done.

In digital marketing, there is no penalty for taking many shots on one goal. We learn quickly and iterate constantly. We expect failure 90% of the time. Make another ad, try another subject line, choose another set of keywords, adjust your budget, tweak the landing page, and so forth. Via many cycles of experimentation, we'll certainly find some winners.

Now that you've got an understanding of how TikTok ads work and you've been creating your 15-second videos, let's figure out how we can further optimize these with the Social Amplification Engine.

With the Social Amplification Engine, optimization is the end goal. It's the final step in the process. How well we can optimize, though, is dependent on the six steps that come before your optimization efforts.

Some of these steps, like digital plumbing, you'll only have to do once. Others, like content, you'll continue working on but we'll show you some helpful methods to get more content out faster.

An 80/20 approach sets all of these elements in order, so that your conversion funnel is well-oiled, fine-tuned, and prepared to convert your customer.

## The Social Amplification Engine

There are 6 phases to Social Amplification.

*Image 5.1: 6 Phases Of Social Amplification*

This system allows you to **maximize what's already working in your business and to increase conversion rates** on existing funnels and find more ideal customers. It's not for brand new products or businesses that don't have an existing funnel.

In **Digital Plumbing** (which you'll learn more about in the next chapter), you build a system that allows you to create remarketing audiences and track your results. With reliable analytics, you can determine where an additional ounce of effort or dollar in ad spend can make the most difference.

Your **Goals** are your metrics and your mission. Metrics are your numerically driven targets - cost per lead, ROI, revenue, website traffic, etc. Your mission must be authentically defined in the WHY of your brand - authentic statements that drive content that converts at each stage of the funnel. These values drive content sequences that effectively drive traffic and conversions.

Your **Content** is tied to these funnel metrics and audience segments - posts to drive ticket/merchandise sales, sponsored content to drive partner activations, videos to drive database growth, etc.

**Target** your content to multiple owned audiences (TikTok remarketing, Google remarketing, email remarketing, app remarketing, tie-ins with your

CRM) and core audiences (lookalike audiences for each conversion type, media/influencer targets, related interest targets).

Putting your Digital Plumbing in place is key to being able to create these audiences and creating cross-channel campaigns (people who've been to your site but haven't bought, who are customers but you don't have their email, have bought last year but not this year, are in your email list but haven't been to the site, etc.).

Once we have established the triad of Goals, Content, and Targeting, we're ready to run ads.

**Amplify** the most important content pieces that will attract the most relevant people and drive engagement; intensify promotional efforts to the engaged crowd for conversions.

Finally, in **Optimization**, we constantly and repeatedly iterate. Stay in the game. Use analytics to determine where to put your additional effort or dollar in ad spend. Expand on working audiences, tweak bidding and creatives where necessary, re-allocate budgets and always measure your performance in terms of your content and targeting against your goals to define success.

---

## PARETO SUMMARY

▷ When it comes to optimizing, we want to learn quickly and iterate constantly.

▷ To optimize your TikTok ads, we use the Social Amplification Engine (maximize what's already working vs. reinventing the wheel)

▷ There are 6 phases to social amplification. 1) plumbing, 2) goals, 3) content, 4) targeting, 5) amplification, 6) optimization.

# Chapter Four:
# Digital Plumbing

*Image 4.1: Social Amplification Phases - Digital Plumbing*

Your first step is to make sure your accounts are set up properly and to make sure that your ads and analytics are in sync. Following this first step will ensure your data is flowing properly and will help you build powerful remarketing audiences to use in your paid efforts.

You will also be able to tell which ads are effective and will feed the right signals into TikTok to give the algorithm the best chance to identify your potential customers.

**One important note:** TikTok ad is still in the early stages of its development and things are changing rapidly. The click-by-click steps and screens we share with you will likely change, but the principles we outline should stay the same and we will do our best to help you understand the principles of what we are saying so you can adapt to those changes.

We will cover 4 topics as we help you get your Digital Plumbing set-up for TikTok:

1. TikTok Business Center
2. Installing the TikTok Pixel
3. Installing TikTok Conversion Tracking
4. Introduction to TikTok Audiences

## TikTok Business Center

If you have had any experience running ads on Facebook, this section will likely feel very familiar. TikTok is doing its best to take the structure that Facebook has created and apply it to its platform.

Much like with Facebook Business Manager, the TikTok Business Center's primary purpose is to allow the business owner to manage assets and the permissions granted to those assets.

## Creating a TikTok Business Center

We have pulled the following steps on how to create a TikTok Business Center directly from TikTok. As the platform evolves, these steps may change but you will be able to find updated steps in the TikTok help center at https://ads.tiktok.com/help.

Step 1: Sign in to TikTok Business Center

1. Go to the https://business.tiktok.com/
   a. You can go directly to the page from your browser, or by clicking the suitcase icon on the top right-hand corner of the TikTok Ads Manager dashboard.
2. If you are a TikTok For Business user but don't have a TikTok ad account:
   a. Click Log In to log in to your account.
   b. Click Enter Business Center once you are logged in.
3. If you are not a TikTok For Business user, you will need to sign up as a new user here: https://ads.tiktok.com/i18n/

Step 2: Create a TikTok Business Center account

1. After logging in, click Create.
2. Name your Business Center and select your time zone.

## Navigating TikTok Business Center

When you first enter your TikTok Business Center you should see a menu on the left-hand side of your screen that will be your primary navigation tool within your Business Center. We'll dive into a few key sections that require a bit more explanation to help you maximize the power of your Business Center.

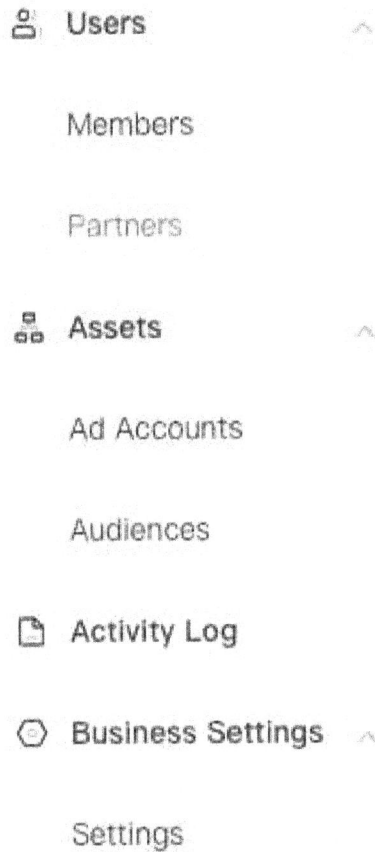

*Image 4.2: TikTok Business Center Left-Hand Menu*

The users' section is the primary place where you will control who has access to your TikTok ad account. There are two categories of users you can create, Members and Partners.

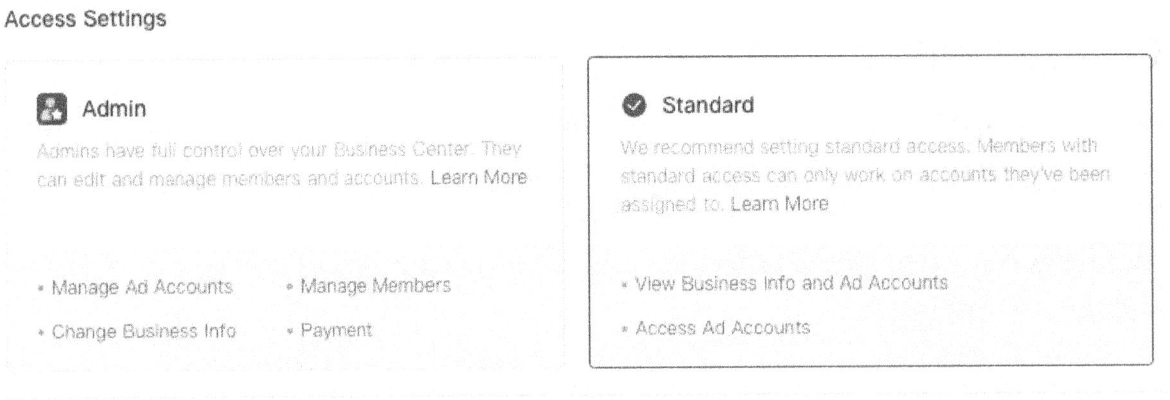

*Image 4.3: Users Section*

## Members

Members should be used when you are granting access to internal members of your team. Members have two types of permissions that you can choose from, Admin and Employee. Admin privileges allow the user to edit everything inside your Business Center.

They can invite new users, create ad accounts, and share your assets. They can also see every asset in your Business Center which gives the flexibility to help run your business. This permission should only be granted to people you can trust and should generally be reserved for team leads or other higher-level team members.

Employee permissions are more restricted. Employees only have access to the assets and abilities you grant to them. They can't invite new users and can only perform the tasks you grant them for each property. This permission level should be used for anyone who needs to work on your ads, but are focused on specific tasks.

### Partners

If you are working with external teams or agencies, you should be sharing your assets using the Partners feature. This allows you to share your assets with another TikTok Business Center, allowing them then assign users to work on your accounts. You still control which permissions these partners can assign, but this takes the burden of managing their team off your shoulders.

### Assets: Ad Accounts

This is where you can see the ad accounts your Business Center owns and has access to. This seems pretty straightforward but there are few nuances that are critical for you to understand here. The key principle for this section of your Business Center is that you want to make sure your business owns your ad accounts. We have seen far too many businesses who have lost ad accounts to rogue agencies or employees and have had to start from scratch.

A key thing to note is that this interface is currently in the process of being changed. The changes are being rolled out slowly, so we will do our best to cover the methods of adding ad accounts to this section, but you may not have all of the options (yet) listed in this book. But they will come.

There are currently three methods for adding a TikTok Ad Account to your Business Center.

1. **Create a TikTok Ad Account:** If you have never created a TikTok Ad account, this is the simplest method to understand. Using this method you will create a new ad account that will be owned by the Business Center. This feature is slowly being rolled out to ad accounts and may not be available to you yet.

2. **Request Access to Ad Account:** This method is unfortunately the one we see work most often, but is not ideal in most cases. When you request access to an ad account, you are gaining access to the account using your Business Center but the ownership of the account remains with the Tiktok profile that created the account. If you are the business owner and created the account, this is not a problem. This becomes more of an issue if one of your employees creates the account with their TikTok profile. Using this method, you will get access but the ownership stays with the original user. If that employee leaves or goes rogue, you risk losing your account.

This also is a problem if an agency creates an account for you and grants you access but keeps the ownership. As a business owner, you should insist that agencies work within ad accounts owned by your business center.

3. **Transfer Ad Account:** This method gives your Business Center access to an existing ad account, but also transfers the ownership of the account to your Business Center. If you or one of your employees created an ad account for you, this is the best method for pulling the ownership of the ad account into your Business Center. Unfortunately, the success of this method has been spotty at times and we have been forced to use the other access methods. If you don't have a ton of historical data in an ad account that will not allow you to transfer ownership, it may be worth starting from scratch with a new ad account to avoid potential headaches down the road.

## Installing the TikTok Pixel

With your TikTok Business Center up and running, you are ready to set up your TikTok tracking. TikTok's tracking system operates similar to the way other social platforms do, with a central tracking pixel to track the behavior of users on your site and extra code snippets to identify specific conversion events and pass extra pieces of information back with those key web actions.

**Pareto Point**

We will start by walking you through the process of setting up your base TikTok pixel using a tool called Google Tag Manager. **Google Tag Manager is a tool that allows you to manage all of your various tracking elements in one place**. It reduces the amount of code on your site which helps improve your site speed and is overall a much simpler way to manage your digital tracking elements.

1. Open your TikTok Ad Account and hover over the Assets section in the menu at the top of your screen. Select Event from the drop-down menu.

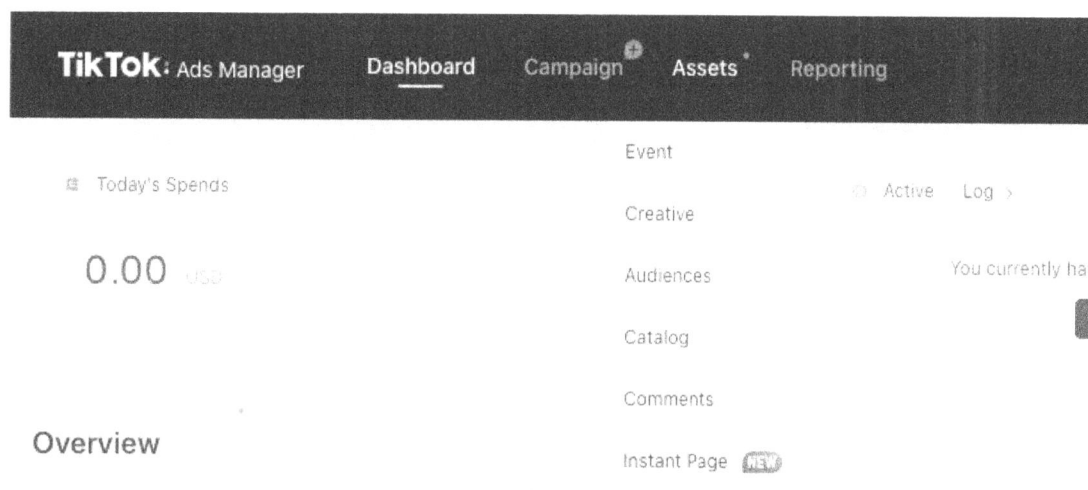

*Image 4.4: TikTok Ads Manager - Assets Dropdown Menu*

2. On the next screen, click on Manage under the Web Events section of your page. You will then be given the option to Create a Pixel.

3. Name your pixel and select manually install pixel code from the Installation Type section. Then click Next.

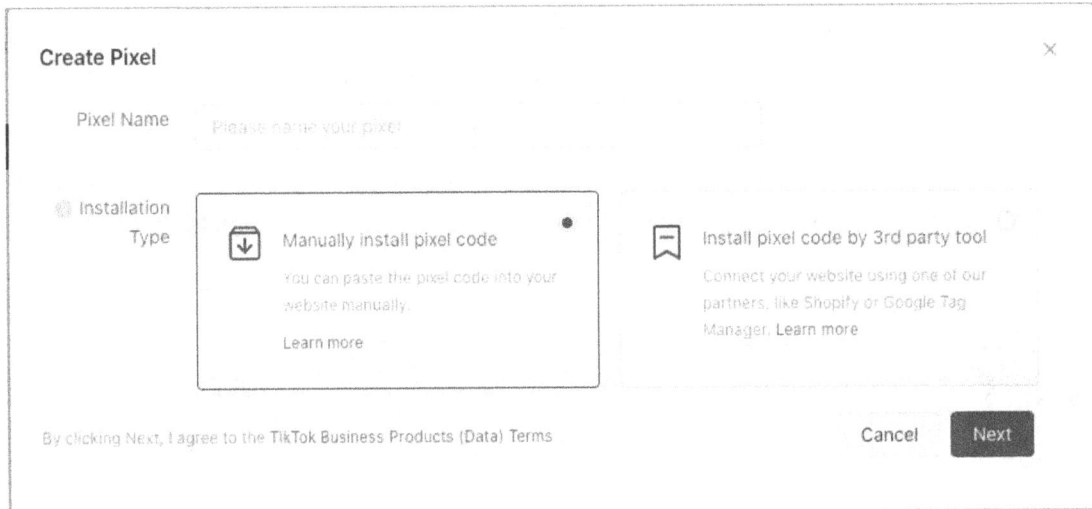

*Image 4.5: Create Pixel For TikTok Business Account*

4. On the next screen, you have a choice between Standard Mode and Developer Mode. Standard mode allows you to use Event Rules within TikTok to create your conversion events. We prefer using Developer mode because that gives us more advanced tracking capabilities and is fairly simple to do with Google Tag Manager.

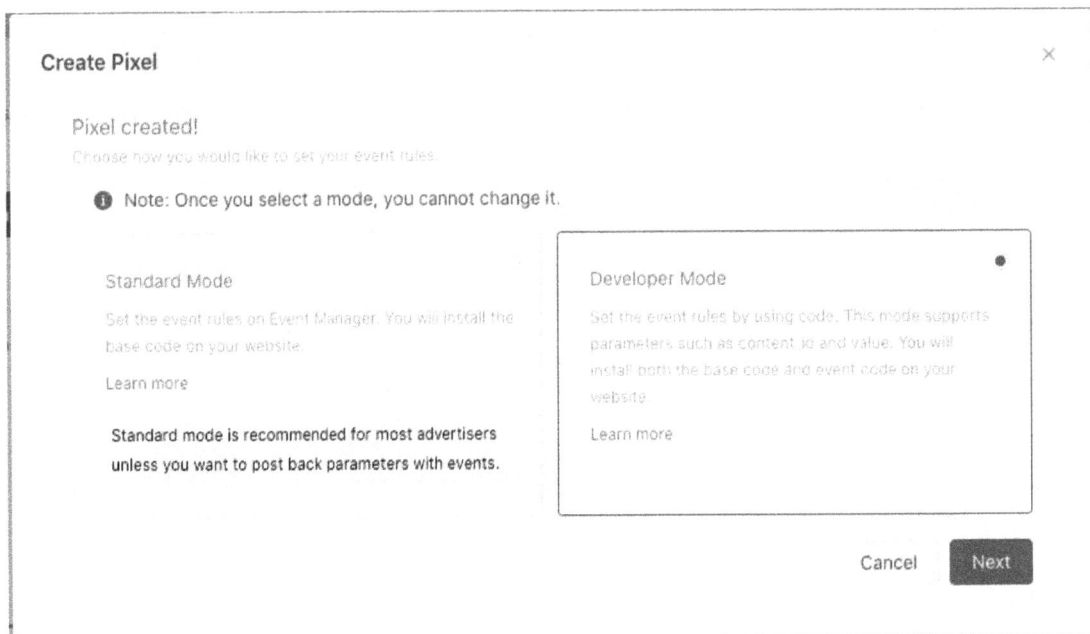

*Image 4.6: Different Modes*

5. On the next screen, you will see the TikTok Pixel code. Click on the code to copy it to your clipboard and then scroll down and switch on the Advanced Matching function for your pixel.

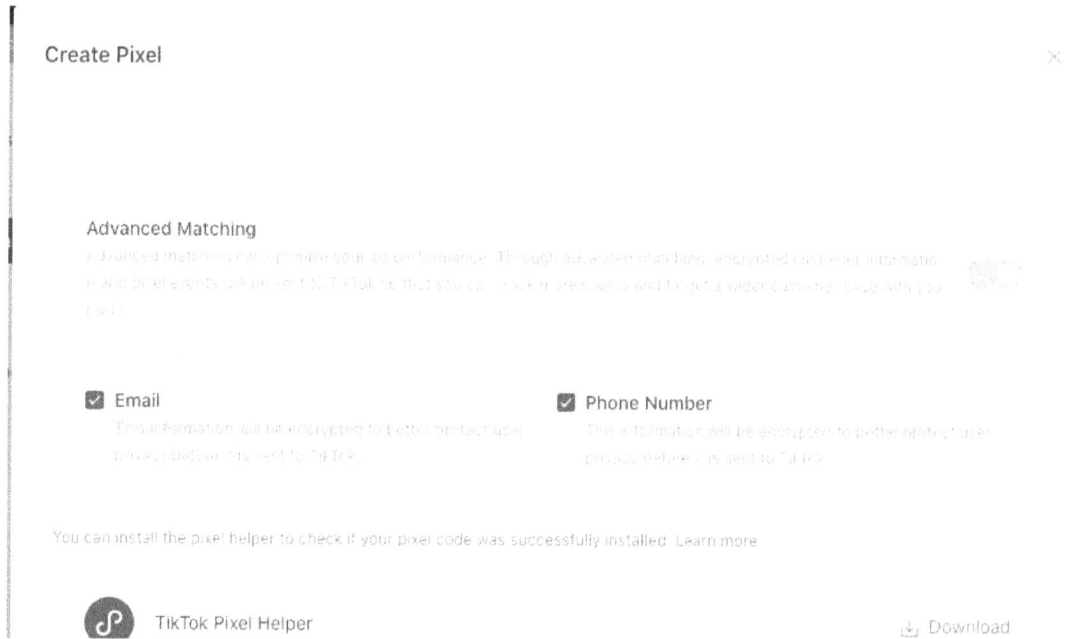

Image 4.7: Advanced Matching

6. In a new tab, open your Google Tag Manager account and click on Tags in the menu on the left-hand side.

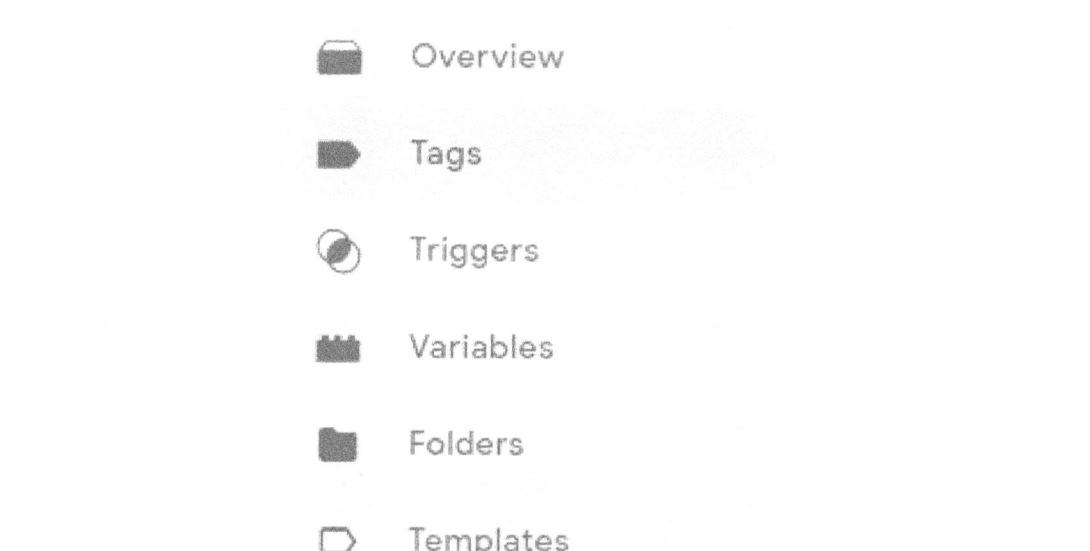

Image 4.8: Google Tag Manager - Tags Menu

7. In the upper right corner of your screen, you should see an option to create a new tag. Name your tag and then click on the Tag Configuration section. Scroll down the list of options available to you and select Custom HTML. In the HTML section provided, paste your copied pixel code.

8. Next, click on the triggering section to open up the list of triggers or rules you can use to fire your tags. This is a base pixel so you want it to fire on All Pages. This is a prebuilt trigger so you can just select it from the list. Once you've completed all these steps your tag should look like this:

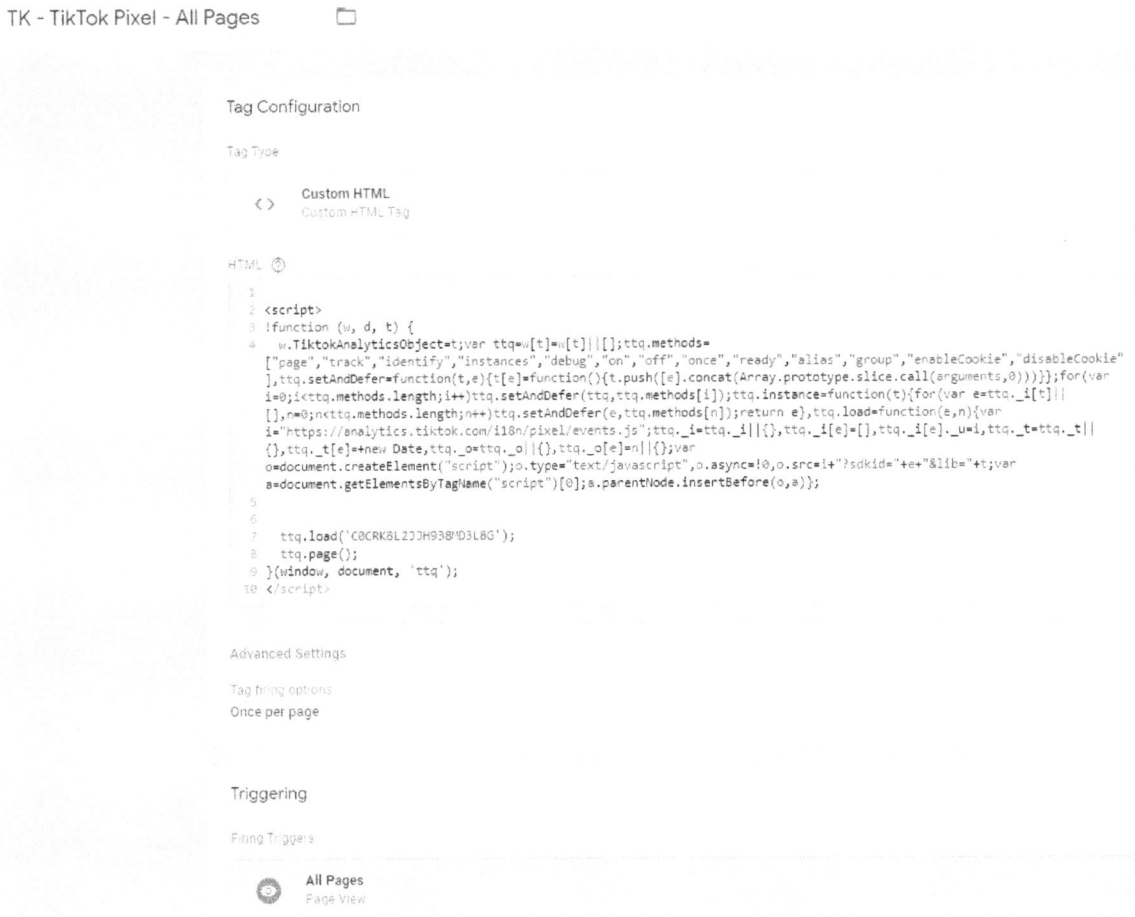

*Image 4.9: Google Tag Manager - Tag Configuration*

9. Click on the Save button in the upper right corner and your TikTok pixel install is complete.

## TikTok Conversion Tracking

With the base TikTok pixel installed on your site, we're now going to move on to conversion tracking. Using TikTok's developer mode you will be creating small code snippets that pass extra pieces of information back to the main TikTok Pixel that indicates when key Business actions have been taken. This mirrors the Facebook pixel very closely so if you have set up conversion events for Facebook before this process will look very familiar to you.

1. Head back to your open TikTok tab and you should have your Events Manager pixel install window open. Just above the Advanced Matching section, you should see a section labeled Event Code and Parameters. In this section, you should see a Learn More Link that will take you to the Event Code page.

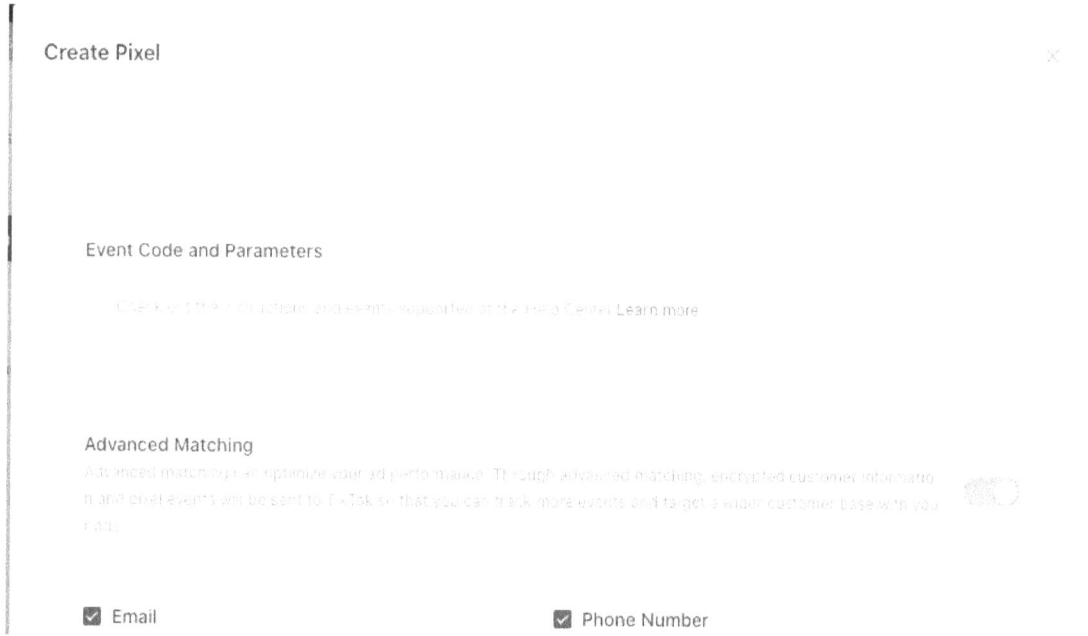

*Image 4.10: TikTok Events Manager Pixel*

2. On this page, you are going to see a table of contents on the right side of the screen. Select 2.3 Pixel Event Code from this list. This will bring you to a table that lists all of the conversion events you can track and send to your TikTok pixel.

| Event | Description | Event Code |
|---|---|---|
| Add Payment Info | When payment information is added in the checkout flow. | ttq.track('AddPaymentInfo') |
| Add to Cart | When an item is added to the shopping cart. | ttq.track('AddToCart') |
| Add to Wishlist | When an item is added to a wishlist. | ttq.track('AddToWishlist') |
| Click Button | When a button is clicked. | ttq.track('ClickButton') |
| Complete Payment | When a payment is completed. | ttq.track('CompletePayment') |
| Complete Registration | When a registration is completed. | ttq.track('CompleteRegistration') |
| Contact | When contact or consultation occurs. | ttq.track('Contact') |
| Download | When a button to open an external browser download page is clicked. | ttq.track('Download') |
| Initiate Checkout | When the checkout process is started. | ttq.track('InitiateCheckout') |
| Place an Order | When an order is placed. | ttq.track('PlaceAnOrder') |
| Search | When a search is made. | ttq.track('Search') |
| Submit Form | When a form is submitted. | ttq.track('SubmitForm') |
| Subscribe | When a subscription is made. | ttq.track('Subscribe') |
| View Content | When a page is viewed. | ttq.track('ViewContent') |

*Image 4.11: Conversion Events*

3. After you have decided which event best matches the action you are trying to track, you can copy the code snippet from the right side column.

4. Click back to your Google Tag Manager tab and click on New in the Tag section to create another new tag. Name your tag and then click on Tag Configuration. This will be another custom HTML tag. You will then need to paste the code you copied from the table in the blank section. You then need to help Google Tag Manager understand what type of code you just added by adding <script> to the front of your code and </script> to the end. Your finished HTML section will look something like this:

```
HTML
1  <script>
2    ttq.track('ViewContent')
3  </script>
4
```

*Image 4.12: GTM Script*

5. With your code snippet implemented, you are ready to set the triggering rules for this conversion event. On your base pixel, you want to have the TikTok pixel fire on every page of your site. On this

conversion event, you are trying to identify a specific action on your site and only send this piece of code when that key action has been completed.

The easiest way to do this is with a Thank You page and this is the method we will show you here, but Google Tag Manager has plenty of options available to you if you want to try more advanced triggering conditions.

6. Scroll down to the Triggering section of your conversion event tag and click to select a trigger. Instead of selecting one of the prebuilt triggers, click on the plus (+) icon in the upper right corner. This will give the option to create a trigger.

7. In the new window, name your trigger and then click on the Trigger Configuration section. This will open a new window showing you all the options for triggers you can create. Select Page View from the menu.

8. Click to select some page views and then click on the dropdown menu on the left of your screen to select how you want to identify the page you want to trigger your event on. We generally like to use page path. In the middle section, select equals and then paste the page path for your Thank You page in the right section.

Your trigger should look something like this:

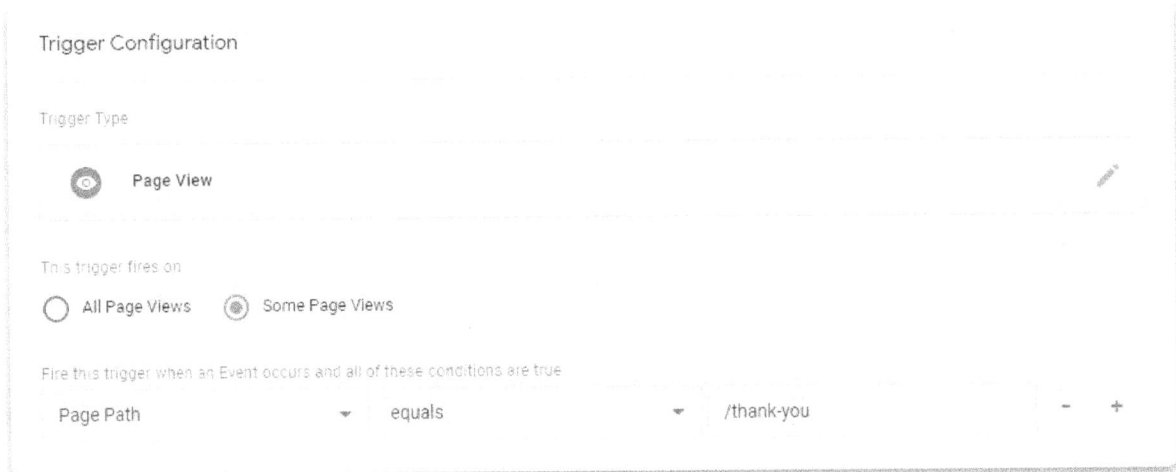

Trigger Configuration

Trigger Type

⊙ Page View

This trigger fires on

○ All Page Views   ◉ Some Page Views

Fire this trigger when an Event occurs and all of these conditions are true

| Page Path | ▾ | equals | ▾ | /thank-you | − + |

*Image 4.13: Trigger Configuration*

9. Click on Save in the upper right corner to save your trigger and then again to Save your Tag. Once these have been saved, you can click Publish in the upper right corner to publish your changes. If your Google Tag Manager is installed on your site, you should see these changes on your site immediately.

## TikTok Audience Types

One of the most important reasons for setting up your digital plumbing is to make sure you have access to all of the various audience types TikTok has to offer.

Though interests and other audience types are fun, **the most powerful audiences are created based on actions individuals take with your content** or on your site demonstrating their interest in your offer.

Installing the TikTok pixel gives you the power to create website remarketing audiences, but there are other audience types we want to briefly introduce you to.

To get to your audience's screen, open your TikTok Ad account and hover over the Assets section, and this time you will select Audiences.

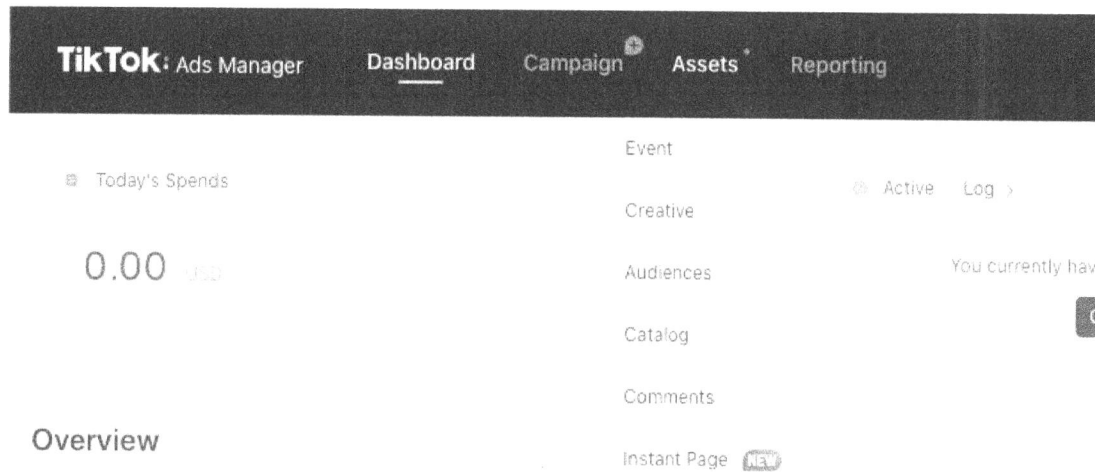

*Image 4.14: TikTok Ads Manager - Assets > Audiences*

If you click on the Create Audiences button on this new screen you will be given two options, Custom Audiences or Lookalike Audiences. Custom Audiences are audiences made up of people who are part of your email lists or who have taken certain actions to interact with your content or your website.

## Custom Audience Types

● Customer File - This audience is created by uploading a list of individuals who have provided their information to your business. Currently, TikTok only accepts lists created using various advertising ids from Facebook, Apple, or Google, but soon you will be able to upload names and emails and TikTok will try to match that information to users.

● App Activity - This audience type uses interactions with your app to create an audience to remarket to. This requires an advanced setup beyond the needs of most business owners.

● Lead Generation - TikTok offers lead forms that can be completed without a user leaving the site. These can be incredibly powerful tools and these audience types allow you to create audiences from people who have interacted with these forms, ranging from people who submitted the forms to people who just opened them but did not fill them out.

● Engagement - This audience is created from people who interact with your paid or organic video on Facebook. You can target based on views, impressions, or a combination of these various options.

● Website Traffic - This audience type is built from your TikTok pixel and is based on site activity including URL rules you set or conversion events you have installed.

## Lookalike Audiences

Lookalike audiences are a powerful audience type that takes a set group of people commonly referred to as a seed audience and then finds a larger group of people who are similar to that original group. Generally, you want to use high-value audiences as these seed audiences to ensure you are building an audience that is similar to your most valuable customers. The most common seed audiences are lists of past or current customers, but you can get creative in what you use to generate these audiences.

### Event tracking and attribution

You should also install the TikTok Pixel Helper Chrome Extension, this helps verify that the Pixel was embedded correctly, and in troubleshooting, if for some reason it's not capturing/firing when it should be. This is very similar in nature to the Facebook pixel helper.

## Final Business Account Steps

Part of the process you need to go through to get your business verified, just like in Facebook. Without completing this step, you won't be able to run TikTok ads, so it's important that you do this as soon as possible.

Start by either creating a new TikTok business account (what we just covered above) or converting your personal account to business. Don't forget to register it.

Converting your personal account has pros and cons. With business accounts, you can run ads, but you can't use commercial music (which contributes to some of the most viral posts). The upcoming benefits of registering your business are not fully clear yet, nor are penalties for not registering.

As part of registration, you do have to put in your tax ID number and a business document (I use the W9), which is similar to businesses registering on Facebook.

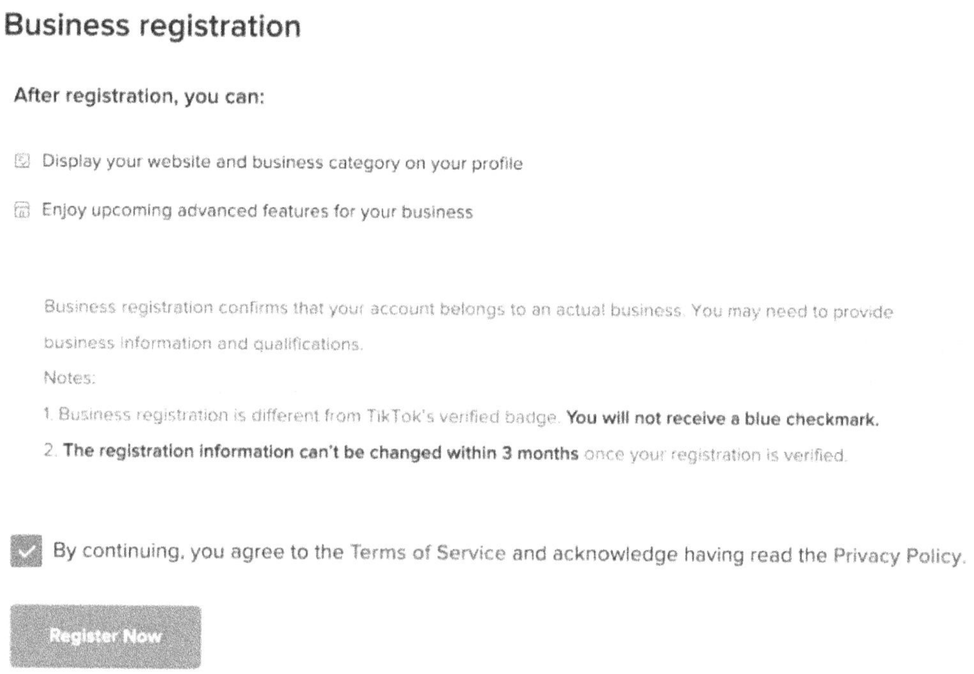

**Business registration**

After registration, you can:

- Display your website and business category on your profile
- Enjoy upcoming advanced features for your business

Business registration confirms that your account belongs to an actual business. You may need to provide business information and qualifications.

Notes:

1. Business registration is different from TikTok's verified badge. **You will not receive a blue checkmark.**

2. **The registration information can't be changed within 3 months** once your registration is verified.

✓ By continuing, you agree to the Terms of Service and acknowledge having read the Privacy Policy.

Register Now

*Figure 4.15: TikTok Business Registration*

We'll be focusing on in-feed ads only when running TikTok ads. They are the best (aka the 80/20 of the ads available that bring in the results we're looking for) for professional businesses.

(You can learn all about in-feed ads here: https://tinyurl.com/tiktokinfeed.)

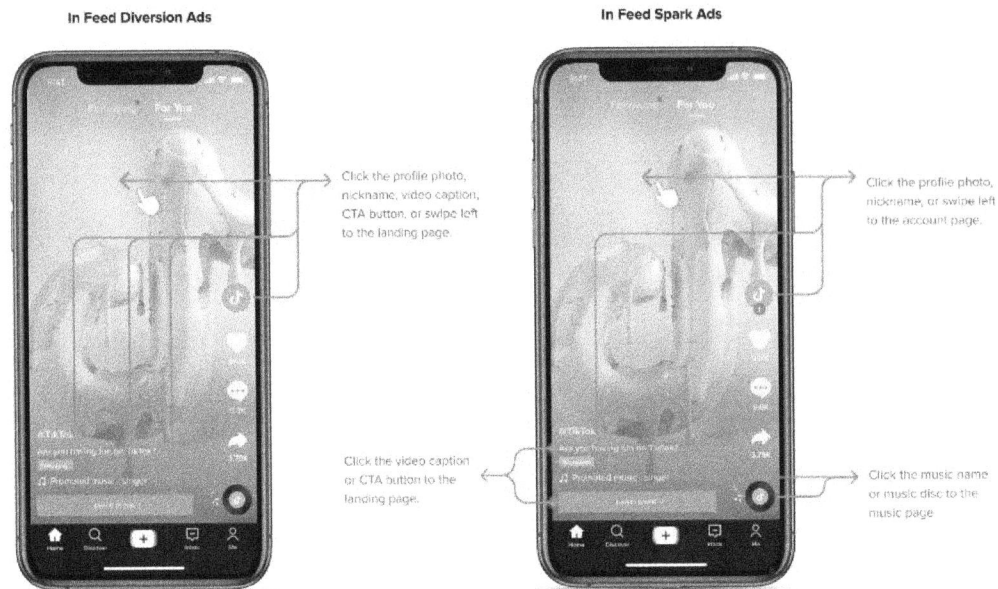

*Image 4.16: How In-Feed Ads Are Accessed/Shown*

**This last point is key, so pay attention: most of the engagement on your ads will be from mobile, not desktop.** But you will manage the ads from your desktop. Technically, we can run some basic ads (like a boosted post) on mobile, but there is no true ads interface for mobile.

Your videos will need to be optimized for mobile. This is why we encourage you to record your videos with your smartphone in the first place.

## PARETO SUMMARY

▷ Digital Plumbing is where you build your audiences and track your results. With reliable analytics, you can determine where an additional ounce of effort or dollar in ad spend can make the most difference to your ROI and sales.

▷ TikTok's Business Center is similar to Facebook's Business Manager.

▷ TikTok's pixel tracking is like other social media platforms.

# Chapter Five:
# 80/20 Economics For TikTok Ads

Economics is the most critical aspect of marketing because you can have both the best customer list and the best sales pitch in the world, but if your pricing strategy is lousy you'll still go broke.

Bad economics means you're taping dollar bills to every product that gets shipped out the door. Better marketing only hastens your trip to the bankruptcy court.

The question you need to be asking and answering is: *How much **value** does the customer get?*

Economics should always be the starting point of any marketing conversation. Especially if you're searching for breakthroughs and not just minor improvements.

**Here's a handy rule of thumb:** 80/20 says that 20 percent of the people will spend 4 times the money. It also says that 4 percent of the people will spend 16 times the money. Memorize this—it's one of the most powerful facts you could ever know about business.

The "Principle of the $2700 espresso machine" says that for every 1000 people who will spend $5 on a latte, one of them will spring for a gleaming stainless steel $2700 espresso machine. Total revenue of $7700 instead of $5000, and the additional comes from one person *who was already a buyer*. No new customers are needed.

The 80/20 principle says this is almost as reliable as gravity. It radically changes the economics of any business and makes it far easier to profitably acquire new customers.

It doesn't matter if it's insurance, metal stampings, or jet airplanes; a "gourmet" version is always possible. This can transform the entire industry.

Something to think about as you move through this chapter.

## What's Your TikTok Ads Goal?

Looking back at the Power Triangle, the economics depends on what your goal is with your TikTok ads.

Are you looking to convert viewers into email list subscribers?

Then the economics would be what your audience gets in exchange for their email address and the value of that email address to your business.

Are you focused on selling your offer and turning leads into customers?

Then the economics would be what your audience paid to purchase your offer and the value of that purchase to your business.

Remember, we want to follow this rule of thumb when we're looking at economics: *80/20 says that 20% of the people will spend 4 times the money. It also says that 4% of the people will spend 16 times the money.*

So how can we optimize your ROI (return on investment) further?

There are a few areas we can look to apply the 80/20 rule of thumb from the perspective of where your TikTok ads lead to.

1. Your content and
2. Your owned audiences.

We can narrow in a little further though.

Within your content, we can amplify the most important pieces of content that will attract the most relevant people and drive engagement; intensify promotional efforts to the engaged crowd for conversions.

We can create lookalike audiences for each conversion we want to optimize for as well as ensure that we have strong automation within your CRMs.

## Breaking Down Your Goals

BUSINESS PACKAGES — 1 PLUMBING — 2 GOALS — 3 CONTENT — 4 TARGETING — 5 AMPLIFICATION — 6 OPTIMIZATION

With your digital plumbing foundations set up, you are ready to clarify and solidify your goals on TikTok. For your purposes, goals are the combination of the metrics you are looking to achieve and your mission and purpose as a company. As a baseline, we generally recommend you decide on the following steps as part of your Goal setting process:

- Define your mission (start with your WHY) and identify your desired outcome and customer segments
- Identify your primary goals in the next 90 days
- Determine your target Cost Per Acquisition (CPA) and Return On Ad Spend (ROAS)
- Determine your ads budget relative to campaign goals (optimizing for clicks, page likes, form submissions, etc.)

**Finding Your Why**

Many people have spent time explaining how to identify your mission or why in life so we won't spend much time covering those methods here. If you haven't taken the time to identify this purpose for yourself and your business, we strongly recommend that you do so now as part of setting your goals for TikTok.

Though the metrics of profit and spend are important, if you don't make a personal connection with the individuals your content reaches, you will struggle to find success on TikTok and social media in general. Establishing a central mission or purpose for yourself and your business lays a foundation on which you can build those personal connections.

**Selecting Your Key Metrics**

Every business has slightly different needs and goals when they start advertising on TikTok. An important step before you start spending money on ads is to identify what key metrics mean you have succeeded on TikTok. You may even have multiple metrics for different stages of your TikTok funnel.

For example, if I want to increase my brand awareness, I might want to look at how many video views I can generate and at what cost. If I'm looking to sell products, I'm concerned about revenue, ad spend, and return on ad spend.

Generally, advertisers divide their efforts into three distinct steps or stages often referred to as Awareness, Consideration, Conversion. You may decide to use TikTok for just one or for all three of these advertising stages. Below we have listed a few common metrics business owners may want to look at in each of these stages.

**Commonly Used Metrics**

| Awareness | Consideration | Conversion |
|---|---|---|
| • Video Views | • Clicks | • Purchases |
| • Cost Per Video View (CPV) | • Cost per Click (CPC) | • Cost per Acquisition (CPA) |
| • Engagements | • Click-Through Rate (CTR) | • Leads |
| • Cost Per Engagement (CPE) | • Leads | • CPL |
| • CPM (Cost per 1000 people impressions) | • Cost per Lead (CPL) | • Return on Ad Spend (ROAS) |
| | • Landing Page Views | |

**TikTok Specific Considerations**
The above metrics are good overall benchmarks, but for TikTok, you also want to consider the following:

• CPMs vary from $2 to $10, depending on engagement rate and targeting, much like Facebook.

• 10% engagement rate (likes/impressions) is a good organic or paid benchmark not just on TikTok, but all platforms. A "killer" TikTok can get 35% engagement, which drives the effective cost per like down to 3 cents.

• View-through rates (impression to view) is higher on TikTok, since they count a view at 2 seconds (or less) instead of a standard 3 second view. So getting over 50% here is good.

• High video completion is more important than low engagement rate. Shorter video means better completion rate, so tightly edit the hook and eliminate dead air.

● Cost per follower on TikTok is much like cost per fan on Facebook — expect 10 cents for viral categories (entertainment, fashion, sports) and north of $5 for unsexy (B2B, SaaS, enterprise/industrial).

**Pareto Point** The easiest and highest ROI is from remarketing of web and email traffic. So the more volume you have already on your site and the better your ads are doing in other channels, the stronger your remarketing performance will be on TikTok.

Everyone knows remarketing has the highest ROI but small volume. This is why we extend to lookalikes and also untargeted traffic to really scale this further.

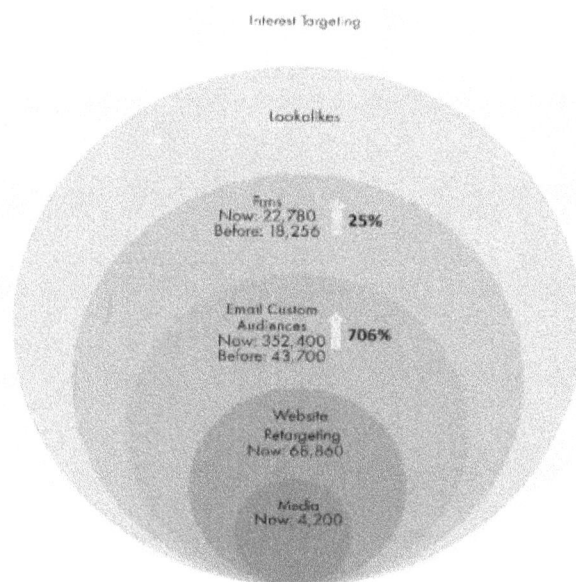

Interest Targeting

Lookalikes

Fans
Now: 22,780
Before: 18,256    **25%**

Email Custom
Audiences
Now: 352,400    **706%**
Before: 43,700

Website
Retargeting
Now: 66,860

Media
Now: 4,200

*Figure 5.2: TikTok Audience Performance*

These concentric circles show how we visualize our retargeting campaigns. Each circle represents moving from one targeted audience to another. We start each campaign with core customers and influencers and then grow to expand to other profitable audiences based on how they relate to the business.

## PARETO SUMMARY

▷ Economics... **Here's a handy rule of thumb:** 80/20 says that 20 percent of the people will spend 4 times the money. It also says that 4 percent of the people will spend 16 times the money. Memorize this— it's one of the most powerful facts you could ever know about business.

▷ The easiest and highest ROI is from remarketing of web and email traffic. So the more volume you have already on your site and the better your ads are doing in other channels, the stronger your remarketing performance will be on TikTok.

▷ You need to set clear goals for your ads so you know when they are working and when they need to be tweaked.

# Chapter Six:
# Generating Your Content

*Image 6.1: Social Amplification Phases - Content*

The old saying that content is king is never more true than on TikTok. The almighty algorithm-god has shown to be less concerned with battery life than delivering users content that they are most interested in. To put it bluntly, if your content doesn't match up, you won't succeed.

One of the biggest challenges people face when building a content strategy is knowing where to start. It can be tempting to try to sit down and pencil out a huge master funnel with each piece of content. It can be easy to get bogged down in the details and never actually make any videos. Though it is important to have some sort of plan, it is far more important to just start. Because of the nature of the TikTok platform, you don't need some highly edited masterpiece content. You can see huge results with simple videos filmed on your smartphone.

## Review your existing funnels

Let's start with your existing funnels. Do you know your metrics? Your engagement rates, particularly on video?

Remember, we want to amplify what's already working when we get started with TikTok ads.

And if you've been paying attention, you'll likely have guessed that you can replicate what you're doing on platforms like Facebook and Instagram here too.

1. Make a note of the best performing pieces of content (by engagement) in the last 30 days and 90 days.

2. Make a note of the best performing ads (by reach and result) in the last 30 days and 90 days too.

This will give you a good base to start with.

**Don't forget your customers**

When thinking about the content currently working for you, don't forget how powerful customer stories are to a business's content strategy.

Pareto Point

Customer stories on TikTok often provide a greater ROI than hiring an influencer to make short videos for your brand.

Remember, people aren't typically looking for advertisements on social media.

They want to be entertained. When people see a celebrity hawking a product, their immediate thought is they're being sold to, and they're right.

With TikTok, everyone's an influencer.

A customer story, if done right, has more plausibility than someone with a million followers. It's a testimony to a problem your business solved.

What we want to do is create videos that are not too polished, not too professional, but are raw and real. This is something some people in the TikTok community call "Flawsome" (flaws and awesome).

Pareto Point

It's much better to have a mobile video of a customer (or you) walking and talking, like in a conversation with a friend, than to spend your ad budget on something that looks like it came off a television set.

You need to embrace the flawsome.

## The Content Factory

The goal of The Content Factory is the abundant reuse of winning content (yours and that of your customers).

For example, by systematically collecting positive mentions as part of an ongoing operation, we do not have to "make ads" or "come up with ideas." We are using TikTok as the ultimate word of mouth machine to amplify what people are already saying about us.

This extends to being on podcasts, having a book, speaking on stage, interviewing partners, and other ways to "build authority," which is what we push to cold audiences and to help warm audiences convert. But the high authority content is more for experts who already have a converting funnel.

On "hot" social networks like TikTok, authority is especially important. Most influencers define this as showing off a successful lifestyle, speaking on stage, being with celebrities, and so forth.

For reaching young adults, this authority translates to something more like a popularity contest - where they follow the top people in their industry like a social network tabloid.

For us professionals, we would demonstrate our authority with whatever is superficially visually impressive to people in our niche.

We want to give that winning content a megaphone (through social amplification) and have it keep working until engagement peters out or we need to make new updates to keep it fresh.

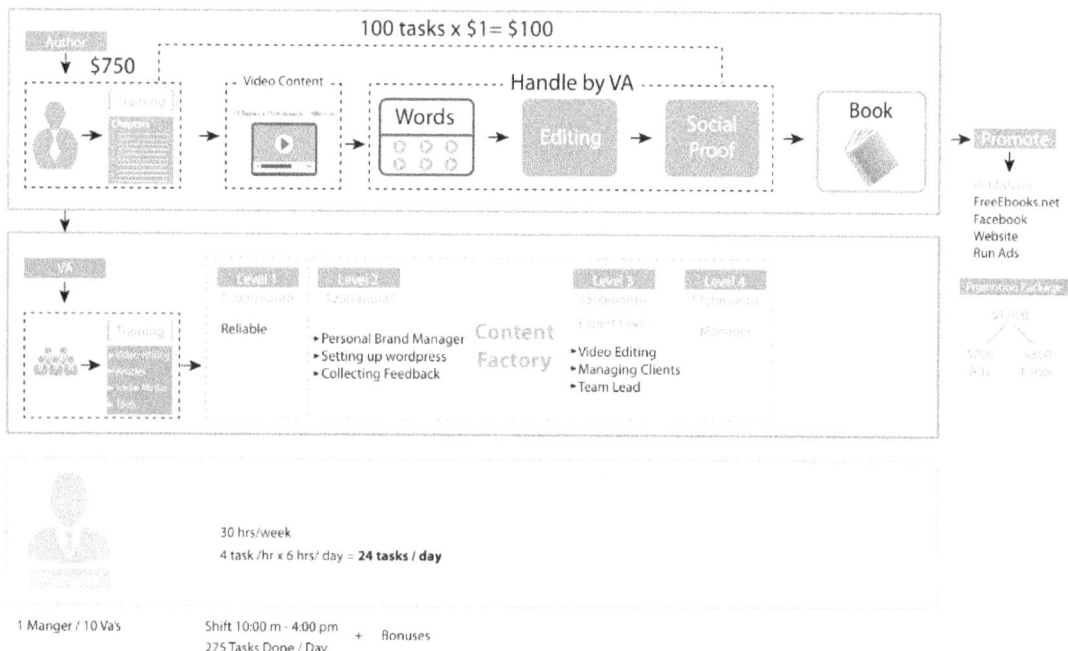

*Figure 6.2: The Content Factory*

In a factory, we have the business owners that create the strategy and systems to allow workers to build products more efficiently. We have managers who oversee each stage of production. And we also have the workers that use tools and machines to help refine the raw materials coming into the factory into products, and then after production, distribute those refined products to customers.

In the Content Factory, the raw material is your raw video. We've talked a bit about what makes great content to repurpose, and we mentioned that customer stories in particular are great pieces of content to reach your target audience.

You can take that raw material–a long-form video, a short customer story, or another piece of content that is working well for you on social media–and break it up into short 15-second snippets by having your workers process it, using the tools and systems you have in place.

But what's great about The Content Factory is that one piece of raw video material does not just have to serve one purpose.

With the right tools, systems, and workers in place, you can edit the long-form video to put it on YouTube, create blog posts to put on your site, extract audio to turn it into a podcast, transcribe it and turn it into social media posts, and also have tons of TikTok videos to continue engaging your audience.

## Content Planning

### Topic Wheel

Social media is all about word of mouth and social proof. This is especially important on TikTok as **the people or things in your video have an impact on who your video reaches** and its number of impressions. The TikTok algorithm is incredibly smart. We have seen people repeat the same words with different objects in the background and those videos have reached vastly different audiences.

A Topic Wheel is a method of planning and thinking about the topics important to your business. It's for brainstorming all the people you could reach out to who care about those topics.

By building a network of high authority individuals who care about the topics important to you and your business, you start to influence who sees your videos.

A Topic Wheel is fantastic for building evergreen content that is triggered by user action—lead magnets, autoresponders, inbound marketing efforts, SaaS/recurring products, and software companies. This technique is excellent at building loyalty because it amplifies word of mouth into sales by collecting what customers or other high authority subject matter experts are saying about you and distributing their words.

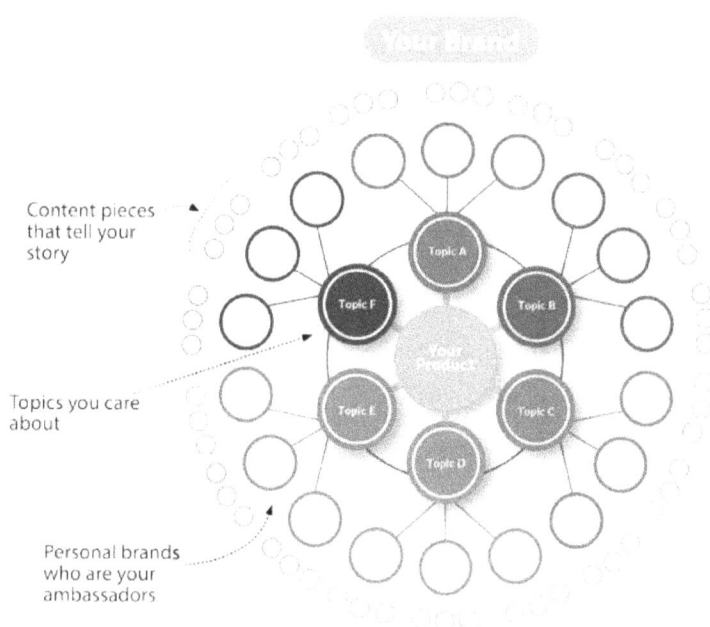

*Image 6.3: Topic Wheel*

**Spontaneous Content**
Spontaneous content is really where the rubber meets the road. This content is the easiest to produce and gives you many opportunities to interact with your target audience. It also gives you frequent shots on goal to find a winner. TikTok is full of videos where the creator simply grabs their phone and creates something, with very little editing or adjustment.

Don't be afraid to take your phone and just get going and encourage other members of your team to do the same. This type of content is often the most personal because people get to see who you are and can make personal connections with you and with your story. Your goal doesn't have to be becoming an influencer. Showing the human element to your business fosters trust and will help your business grow.

 We believe in a combo of a content calendar, the Topic Wheel, and spontaneous (news + curation) content working together. Most companies do just one of the three models of content production, but you'll have greater power when you combine all three.

## Types of TikTok Ads

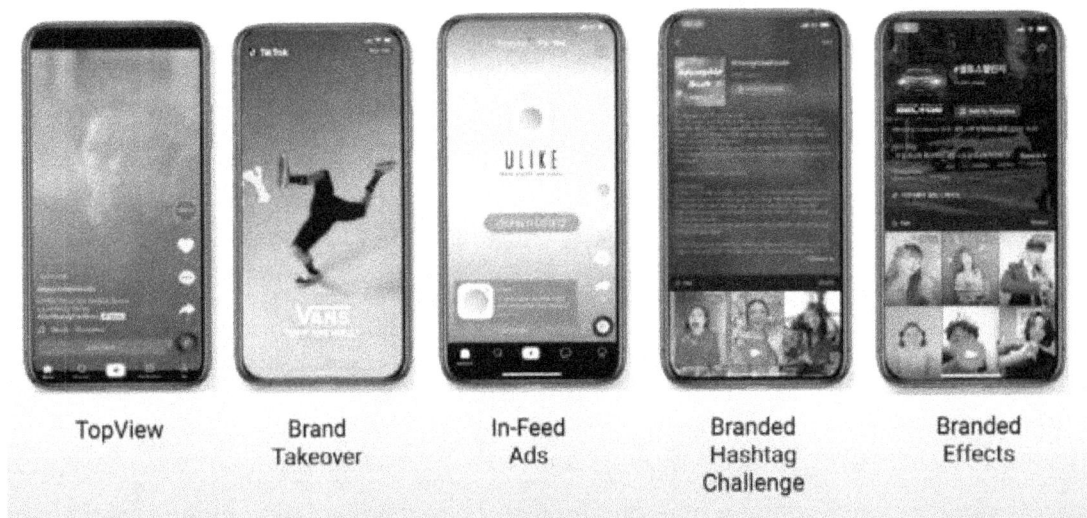

*Image 6.4: Tiktok Advertising Formats*

TikTok has several ad types with varying levels of complexity and ease. If you are a TikTok user, you have likely seen many of these formats before. Though each of these has a place, we focus on In-Feed Ads, especially for small businesses just getting started. These ads are often the cheapest and are almost always the simplest to create.

These ads are also incredibly effective because when done right they can blend into the native feed that TikTok users are already on. If you understand your audience and follow some simple content suggestions, your ads won't look out of place. They will fit into the experience and will be much more effective because they don't break the immersion.

# Different Types of Content

One common thing we hear from clients and others trying to get started on TikTok is that they don't know what types of content to create. Understandably, they don't have time to learn the latest dance trends and even if they did, those types of content may not help their business.

Though there is plenty of room to get creative, we've compiled a few different types of content that are relatively easy to make and can help direct your content creation process. This is by no means an exhaustive list but should give you a good starting point if you aren't sure where to start.

1. Why, How, What Videos
2. Day in the Life/Behind the Scenes Videos
3. Testimonials, Reviews, and Case Studies
4. Related News + Curation Type Content

## Why, How, What Videos

For years we have employed the practice of creating why, how, and what videos that we've used across each new social media platform that has popped up. These videos are simple and are excellent at building trust and connection with your target audience.

*Why Videos* are designed to create awareness and let potential clients know about you. Common examples include a testimonial, the issues you see in your space, why you became x, your mission, or a life-changing moment.

*How Videos* should create consideration and provide value not directly tied into your

sale/offering. You have to be a bit creative here to find ideas that connect to your business, but some examples we have seen are videos covering stretching routines, supplement recommendations, getting proper sleep, running techniques, and podcasts/interviews with other leaders.

*What Videos* are where you make your offer. They create conversions by showcasing your services and utilizing call-to-actions. Share some info or story about your product then invite people to contact you. Share a testimonial with a call to action. This is where you highlight what makes you unique and invite the audience to check it out.

Think of these three video types as categories for your various types of content and a guide on how you introduce yourself to potential customers. You don't propose on the first date so you shouldn't start selling on the first contact you have with a potential customer.

Sorting your content into each of these three buckets can help you maintain balance in the types of content you are creating. The other types of content we will discuss in this section can and should be sorted into these different categories. We generally recommend having at least 3 of each type of video.

As you start testing your videos, you will find videos that flop. That is unavoidable. Even the best content creators have videos that fail. By creating a 3x3 grid of Why, How, What videos, you can employ a testing strategy where you remove the lowest performers and replace them with a new video to fill in your grid. This keeps you balanced and will help you build a library of high-performing content you can have live evergreen in your ad account.

# 3X3 VIDEO GRID

*Image 6.5: Why, How, What 3x3 Video Grid*

## Day in the Life/Behind the Scenes Videos

These videos are great candidates for spontaneous video creation. Showing some of the processes behind your business can be a great way to capture attention and can be done on any given day.

One of our clients sells different types of trees you can plant in memory of loved ones who have passed on. They have a beautiful farm and have had wonderful success with videos taking people on tours of their farm and showing the processes they go through in preparing their gifts for shipping them around the country.

Even if you don't have a gorgeous magnolia grove to stroll through, these behind-the-scenes videos can be a great way to highlight the things that make you and your business unique.

## Testimonials, Reviews, and Case Studies

No one likes the guy at the party who can only talk about themselves. No matter what business you are in, the more you can get your customers or others to talk about your business, the better.

Highlighting the experiences of customers in their own words is one of the best ways to build trust in you and your business. If possible, interview your best customers and ask them what they love about your business. A simple video of them sharing their experience can be one of the most powerful types of content to share online.

If this isn't an option in your industry, you can get similar impacts by creating case studies that highlight the value your business provides. This allows you to highlight the benefits you provide using a concrete example instead of just talking about your offer.

Be careful about mentioning TikTok in your ads, especially in headline text. Just like with Facebook, doing so can lead to ad disapproval. We've not yet seen anyone get banned on TikTok from too many disapprovals. But we can imagine that policy and support differences will narrow over time. For example, TikTok ad support will eventually become as awful as Facebook's.

## Related News + Curation Type Content

This type of content may not be for every business, but if demonstrating authority is beneficial to your business this can be a powerful tool for showcasing your expertise. Videos discussing news related to your business and sharing your opinion are simple to make and provide an opportunity for you to become a trusted figure for potential customers.

TikTok has a feature where you can "stitch" your video response to another video on the platform, allowing you to respond. If you find people discussing your industry on TikTok, film a quick response furthering the discussion and post it. This content will be seen by people who have demonstrated interest in the topic and will help introduce you and your business to potential customers.

## The Perfect TikTok Ad

Let's take a look at the perfect TikTok ad. In image 6.6 you can see what works best.

*Image 6.6: Ideal TikTok Ad*

What makes this the perfect ad?

It shows the person's face, there is motion, which grabs the attention of someone scrolling, it's filmed on a cellphone and is in the preferred 9x16 format. It also includes a text headline so people immediately know the topic, cementing their attention.

For "influencers" that sing, dance, or do athletic stunts, having a text headline isn't necessary. But for professionals who are sharing their expertise, a **text headline is a must**.

To add to this, you'll also want to have the following in place:

- Your video should be 15-23 seconds long
- Have a variety of scenes (or change of scenery)
- Closed captioning turned ON
- Call to action text
- Any type of audio that supports the message you're trying to convey

You need a constant stream of content to target your audience and feed your TikTok ads, and The Content Factory makes this much easier.

You're probably thinking that it's going to take a lot of time to do this, right? You're likely thinking to yourself, *"Dennis has a large team of people helping him, I'm just a one-person show. How can I keep coming up with fresh, new content each week?!"*

But remember I said at the beginning of the book that we only spend 30 minutes a week creating content.

That's still true, no matter how many people you have to support you in your business. Of course, this doesn't include editing and loading up onto the platform. But the creation process itself, once you know what you're doing, can take you no more than 30 minutes a week.

When you understand that you're creating 15-second videos, you can start seeing how quickly these can come together. And when you're repurposing what already exists (like in The Content Factory) and is part of your proven funnels... that's 80/20 at work right there!

We recommend writing a list of 10 topics and spending 3

minutes on each. If you need to catch your breath, change locations, take a sip of water —then you do it.

Since the vibe of the video is so important — the energy level, background, props, etc., we're not looking to just grind out a ton of videos to "check the box," but have enough "at-bats" to hit a home run. You'll learn more about the *how* of this in the following pages.

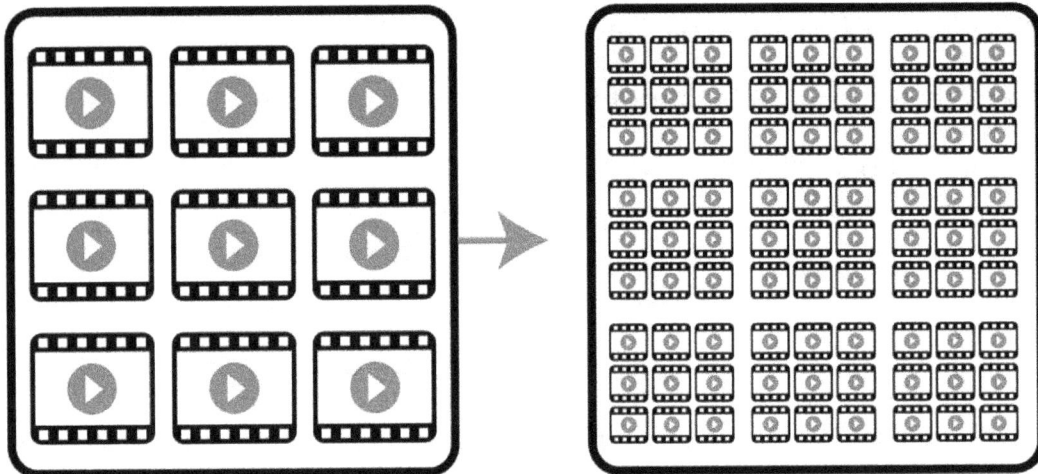

*Image 6.7: One minute videos converted into 15-second TikToks*

## Your First TikTok Video

As far as TikTok ads are concerned, the focus will be on generating video content. Specifically, 15-23-second videos.

You'll focus on content from each of these three categories:

- Why videos
- How videos
- What videos

Start by developing an outline for a 15-second video.

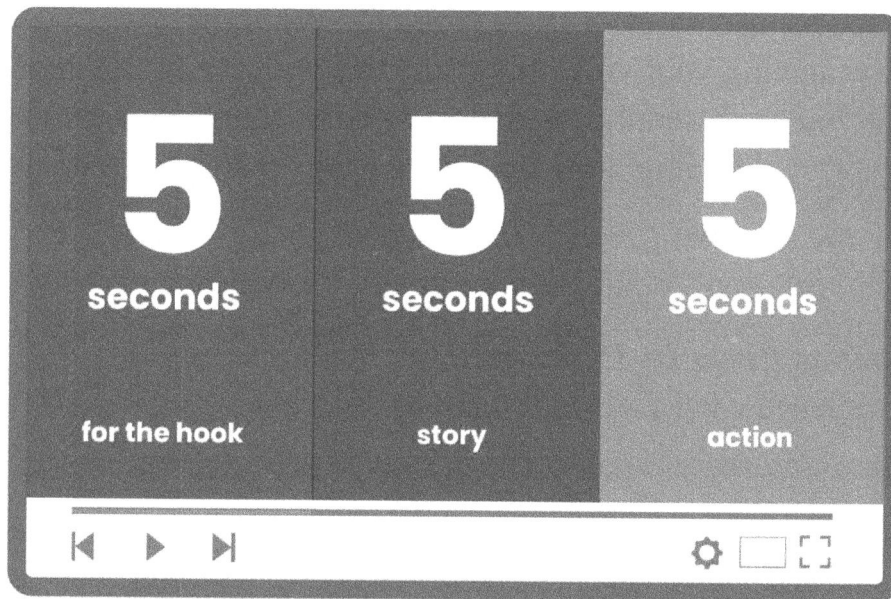

*Image 6.8: Structure of a 15-Second TikTok Video (part 1)*

### *1. Hook (from 0-5 seconds)*

This is where you'll immediately capture the attention of your audience. It's not about you, it's about your audience. No need to say your name or use a "video bumper" here.

Hooks can take the form of a question or statement that provokes curiosity in the viewer. Place the hook as on-screen text and voiceover (by computer voice or yourself) to reinforce it. Because we're using video, a good hook could also be an image of an interesting place, person, or situation. Some examples of effective hooks include:

- "One reason why ..."
- "5 things that X (your target audience)
- "Ever wonder how ..."
- "When I was ..."
- "How to ..."
- "I challenge you to ..."
- Someone off-camera asking an expert a question
- A product unboxing
- A short dialogue with an interesting person
- Provoking curiosity with an interesting prop or setting your videos in an interesting environment

## 2. Ignite pain/pleasure with a story (from 0-5 seconds)

The people watching your video must identify with the problem or opportunity you're presenting. Ask a question or share success stories/failures and highlight the benefit (this needs to be crystal clear).

## 3. Describe the solution (from 5-10 seconds)

What are you offering? What is the product or service?

## 4. Call to action (from 10-15 seconds)

Tell your audience what you want them to do!

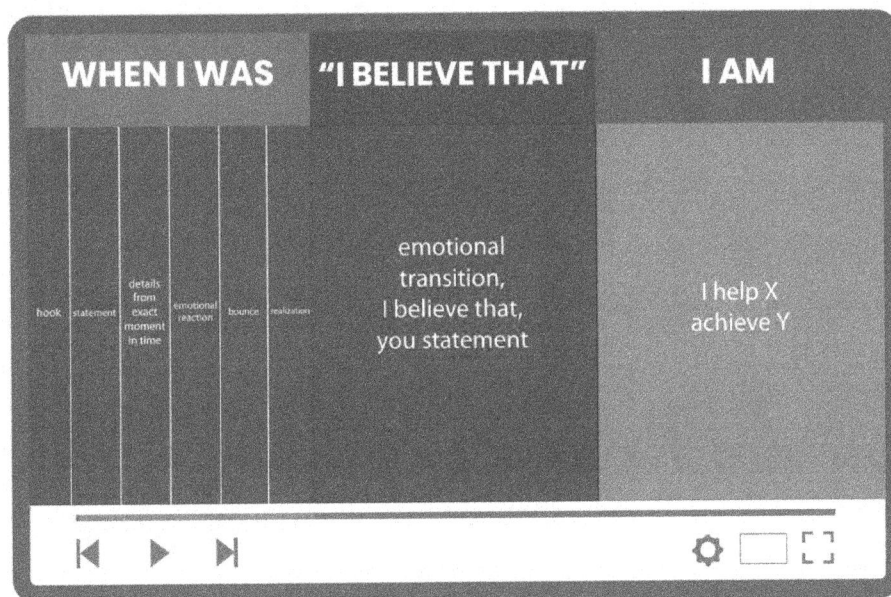

*Image 6.9: Structure of a 15-Second TikTok Video (part 2)*

I like the XYZ model when it comes to generating short videos. You can use a similar template that goes a little like this:

*Improve your golf swing with these three tips.*

*Tip 1*
*Tip 2*
*Tip 3*

*For a customized program to improve your game, give me a call."*

We focus on using simple formats like this because we know they work. You don't need to reinvent the wheel.

In order to be able to create these 15-second videos with ease, you have to know your audience, your brand, and your content inside and out. And if you've done your homework, you'll start by repurposing the content that's already doing well on your other platforms.

## Ads vs. Content on TikTok

It's important to understand the difference between an ad and content at this point as far as TikTok is concerned.

The problem with saying "ad" is that it immediately creates the impression that we're promoting something. You can technically pay for the distribution of your content without directly selling. We call this "social postage" – to have TikTok deliver your content – paying the postage to ensure delivery. This is what we're asking you to do here.

For local businesses that serve a geographical radius such as real estate agents and personal injury attorneys, becoming well-known via TikTok is not hard when we target the city.

**People want to be entertained and surprised on TikTok, not blatantly advertised to**. So providing humor, personality, and some advice relevant to your products/services is how we get a better price on our traffic.

And we can still include a call to action at the end. However, people who like your content will ask questions, look at your profile, and check out your other TikToks.

Need inspiration on where to get started? We've compiled a list of our highest converting 15-second videos for you to review inside the **30-Day TikTok Video Challenge Guide**. **Creating Quality Videos**

Ideally, you'll be using a smartphone purchased within the last 3 years. This will ensure you've got the best camera quality.

Where possible, use natural light. If you're recording your videos inside the house, try and position yourself so that you're standing in front of a natural light source, like a big window.

If you're not able to do this, then you'll need to invest in some lighting equipment. A ring light purchased off Amazon is a good place to start.

It's the little details that matter, which become evident if you put in enough time to notice. For example, on creating iPhone videos to market your business:

• You cannot switch from front to rear camera while filming with the camera. So you either have to use another app or manually flip the phone while in your hand.

• Sound quality is WAY more important than video quality to keep people watching your videos. If you have an iPhone and a regular lavalier mic, you need a TRS to TRRS adapter (2 lines to 3 lines on the plug) and a TRRS to lightning adapter. I use the Rode Wireless Go and have to buy two additional gadgets (the TRS to TRRS adapter and the TRRS to lightning adapter), which don't come in the box. You can use any microphone you wish as long as it connects to your phone, but this is what I use.

• You can share your phone screen if you're a presenter in a Zoom call. And everything works great (just like if you're projecting to Apple TV), except when you're recording video – since the two interfere with each other. So pre-record your videos (stored in your favorite app) or switch to a desktop webcam to show you using your phone.

• Google Photos app is super slow in uploading your videos from the photos library of your phone. So also pay for iCloud, Dropbox, and Amazon Photos (another $10 each per month) to have your videos automatically backed up. You will have to keep these apps open every week to let them catch up since uploads are faster when the app is open.

• Film vertically (portrait mode) most of the time if you're reaching mobile users, but horizontal if it's an interview or you're using a webinar app.

• Amazon Photos has the smartest facial recognition and the easiest way to share groups of pictures (instead of having to select each picture/video one by one) with your external parties (like freelancers and partners).

For your 15 second videos by professionals, we like movement. So walking and talking, other forms of motion — are more interesting than static shots.

You'll always be creating vertical videos. So investing in a selfie stick will help you achieve this with ease.

One of our favorite videos is the "#1 tip" video or the "why" video — where you're walking and talking and sharing one tip. It is the easiest one to do when you're getting started since it's "clickbaity" in a positive way and easy for you to record.

The framework of the "why" video looks like this:

1. WHEN I WAS _____.

Waste no time, get right to the story. This is where the WHY comes in.

2. I BELIEVE THAT _____.

Now go from the emotion of the story you just told to the overarching lesson of what you stand for.

3. I AM _____.

Give a brief explanation of what you do. Make sure to be specific and concise.

You'll see examples of these inside the **30-Day TikTok Video Challenge Guide** too.

**Filming tips**
Where possible, record your 15-second videos in an interesting place, outdoors where possible. We do this so people get to know you, they get to see how your life is, where you live, what you see when you're walking around. It helps your audience see you as a person who is accessible.

Only keep the footage you plan on using in order to save time when editing.

If you're interviewing another person and they are shy or psyched out by the camera, keep the camera running continuously, instead of starting and stopping. This will require more effort on the editing side since you can't clap or motion to unmark sequence starting and endpoints. But your interviewee can comfortably know that they can restart any botched sentences with no pressure to be "perfect."

If they do restart a phrase or sentence, ask them to use a 2-second delay to make it easier on the editing team (or yourself if you're DIYing).

If your equipment allows, ensure that you are doing so in 4k and upload the footage in 4k as well.

Choose or set up the background for your videos to enhance visual aesthetics (i.e. avoid a background that's too cluttered) to help create a far better composition of what you shoot, which will lead to more people engaging in the content. Movement is key, which is why walking and talking is your best option. Being outdoors makes for the perfect background in my opinion.

When uploading in 4k, use Wondershare Converter to easily optimize 4k footage for faster upload. Uploading the footage at this resolution allows you to do punch-ins and much higher quality color correction on the files.

Wondering what a "punch-in" is? A punch-in is when you Zoom into a video. It changes focus, resets attention, and is more interesting. Attention spans are super short on TikTok. So if you try to do a 60-second video just standing there in the same spot, it's unlikely you will hold the audience's attention.

We like to film in 4K (most modern phones do this by default), so when we do a punch-in, we don't lose much resolution – often going down to 1080p.

**Film and edit strategically**
When you're creating Tik Tok videos, keep in mind that you want them to appeal to your target audience. The more you can create this appeal, the more potential your audience will give you the response you want.

Besides creating great content, here are a few other things we can do to increase this appeal:

- **Choose one niche.** Just as with having separate Facebook pages per company or initiative, set up one TikTok business account per business. Have just one theme.

- **Always use background music**. Background music helps to get more impressions. Even if you mute the background music, it still seems to help.

- **If you suck at creating video, use a teleprompter**. The PromptSmart app is a popular one, among many mobile apps that scroll according to how fast you speak.

- **Use compelling text descriptions**. Even though people watch "sound on," the words pre-frame what the post is about, so people don't just swipe past you.

- **Add text to your cover image.** Compelling titles and thumbnails can help your audience anticipate what is to come and encourage them to watch your video to the end.

- **Put in a ton of hashtags**. As spammy as this seems, it still helps the algorithm determine the topic. This is more effective on purely organic posts, as opposed to ones we boost.

- **Use the computer-generated voice**. This isn't for people who don't like how their voice sounds. Most viral videos use the default female voice.

- **Create TikTok stories:** TikTok has a new stories feature where video content expires 24 hours after posting. Combining this type of content with content that is more evergreen can be a good strategy to build a deeper connection with your audience. This is not boostable yet, but we expect it to be in the future.

- **Hire creators.** If you still need some help creating appealing content, reach out to paid influencers that are already on Tik Tok. Tik Tok Creator Marketplace (https://creatormarketplace.tiktok.com/) and #paid (https://hashtagpaid.com/) can help connect your brand with popular content creators already on the platform.

There are also many tactics that people use to increase watch time. Vary these tactics strategically. Don't just use one over and over again.

Here are several you could use:

- Add the on-screen text "Wait for it" with some payoff that happens at the end of the video. (This is still effective but is starting to lose power since it's used too much.)
- Mention a discount code at the end of the video (since we can't fast forward or rewind TikTok.)

Use your hook to create curiosity and drive viewers deeper into the video to understand why the hook was said or done.

---

### If You Want To Make A Viral Video, Model What's Already Working

Chance Rey didn't start out intending to go viral on TikTok. He just wanted to sell more golf balls.

But after only publishing about 15 videos on TikTok, he racked up over 100,000 views for one of his posts and completely sold out all of his merchandise.

Today some of his posts have over 2 million views.

According to Chance, a lot of people overthink TikTok.

**What works for him is modeling**. Look at what's working for others on the site, especially others that are in your niche, and then try to modify that to fit your product and brand.

Once you find out what's working, you want to double down on that, and eventually, it resonates with people.

Chance likes to plan his content out and publish it around the same time each day. He believes that consistent posting during certain hours of the day helps his reach.

Other things that have worked for Chance when creating and editing his videos include:

1. Having a good hook at the beginning

2. Incorporating motion

3. Putting text in the videos

4. Including hashtags

5. Continuing to share posts that do well.

Chance claims anyone can go viral on TikTok, no matter your business niche. If you're modeling other video creators on the platform, you can even turn an industry that seems boring into a viral sensation. Modeling is the trick.

The most important thing, according to Chance, is maintaining a consistent upload of videos. TikTok rewards consistency. On TikTok, engagement and virality are largely a product of learning from others and just continuing to post.

## Uploading Your TikToks

After you've created your TikToks, what's the best way to upload them? Don't post raw videos into the desktop upload, since you can't add as many effects. Use the app on your phone to do this instead.

If you have VAs or a team that has already edited videos, you can schedule posts here. But this also means you're not using TikTok's design elements (big text of the hook and viral music) or the female computer-generated voice.

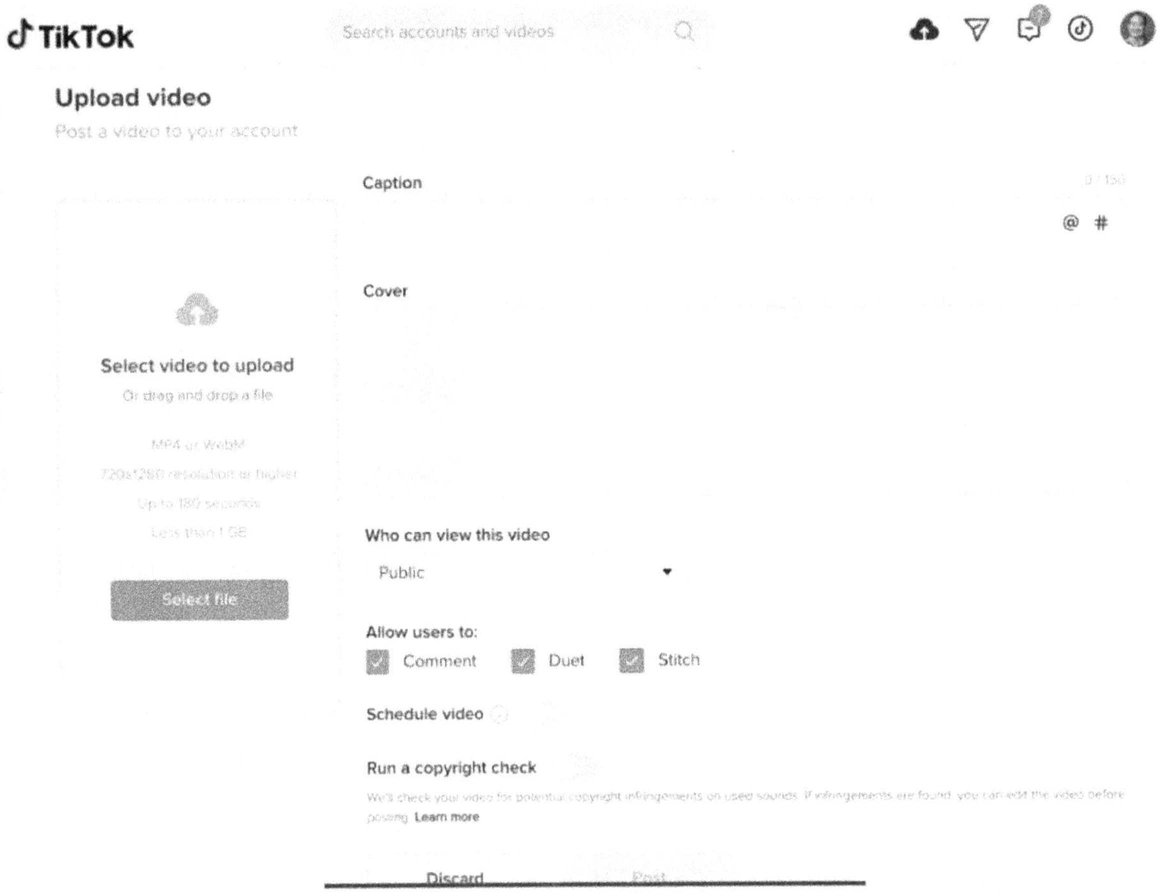

*Figure 6.10: Upload Window on TikTok*

## 15 Seconds of Fame

If you want people to engage your business or your brand, you have to start investing in the currency of digital platforms, attention. People are trading hours of their day scrolling through Facebook and TikTok and you have to fight for every bit of attention you can get. The easiest way to get people's attention is through video. Specifically, 15-second videos. No one is going to watch a 3-minute video if they don't know who you are.

Attention spans on social channels are brief. For example, the average watch time for a video on Facebook is only 6 seconds. You must learn to grab their attention quickly and pull them into the story you are trying to tell. Though you can have a mix of longer 60-second videos, being able to create compelling 15-second videos is critical to catching the attention of your target audience.

This isn't as hard as it seems, you just have to start. So, pick up your phone, point it at yourself and tell us why you're doing the work you're doing. Start with, "when I was..." then tell us, "what I learned..." and finally, "what I believe..." and how that led you to the work you do now.

In this section, we will teach you how to make engaging 15-second videos so you can generate the attention you desire for your brand or business. No one made a good 15-second video on their first try, so start now, make a lot of them. You can test them and compare them, put money behind the winners, and capitalize on your most engaging videos. Before you know it, you'll have hours of content-generating interest for your business or brand.

**Your Mission in 15 Seconds or Less**
If you are following the process we've outlined here, oftentimes the first video a potential customer will see from you is one of your why videos. Your first interaction needs to quickly capture their attention and get them to stop their scroll.

To do this, you need to be able to quickly share a meaningful why in 15 seconds or less. Other videos can stretch to 30 or 45 seconds, but the first touch needs to be quick and powerful. There are three primary components to an engaging why video.

**1. WHEN I WAS____.**

Waste no time, get right to the story. This is where the "WHY" comes in.

**2. I BELIEVE THAT ____.**

Now go from the emotion of the story you just told to the overarching lesson of what you stand for.

**3. I STARTED ____.**

Give a brief explanation of what you do. Make sure to be specific and concise.

*Image 6.11: Three Components Of Engaging Why Video*

Fitting these three components together may seem daunting at first, but don't worry too much. First things first, remember that your first attempt will likely take several attempts before you are satisfied.

By cutting your story down to 15 seconds, you are really being forced to find the most important pieces. You are cutting the fluff and getting down to the heart of your story. This in and of itself is powerful.

When we are creating 15-second why videos, we generally shoot to split the video into three 5 second sections:

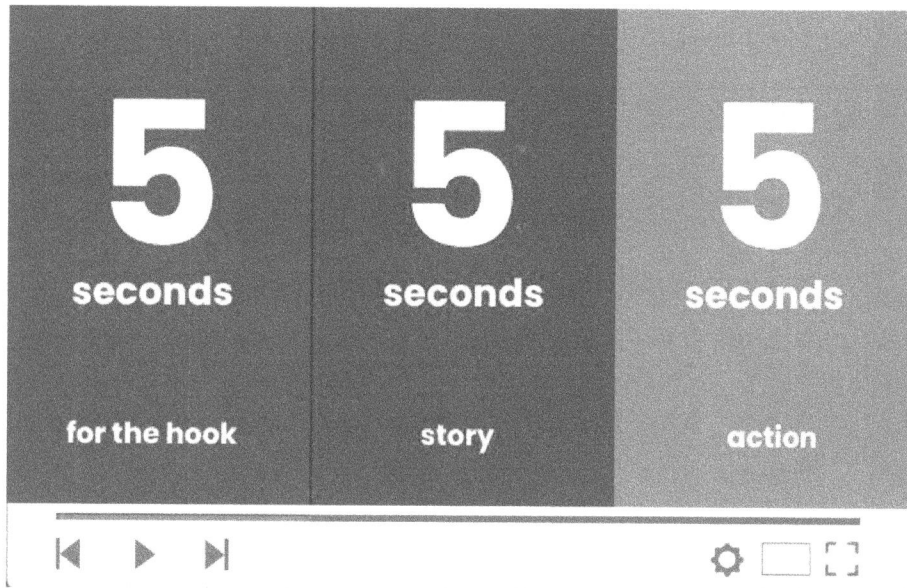

*Image 6.12: Why Video Sections*

If we break this down a little further it looks something like this:

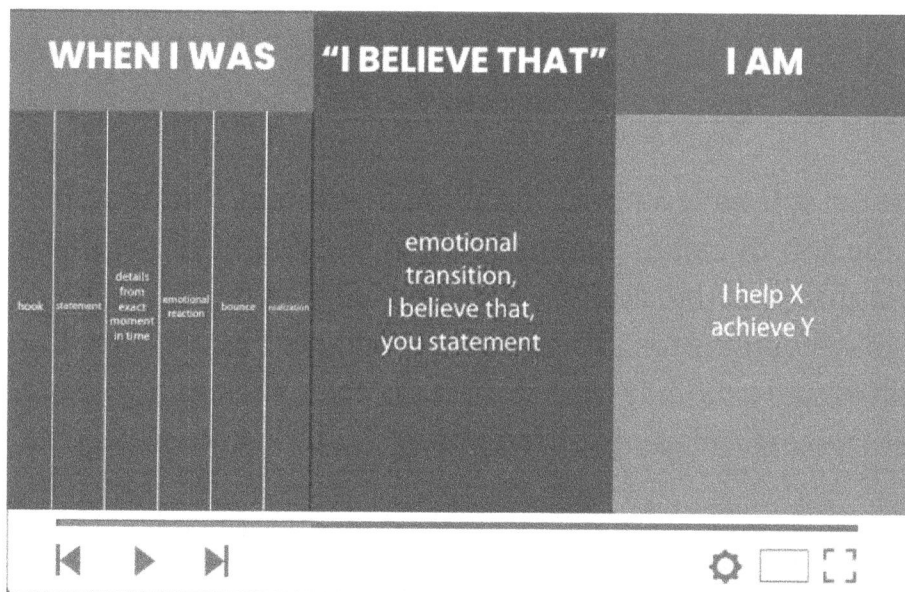

*Image 6.13: Why Video Break Down Sections*

You have to be efficient to fit all of those pieces in 15 seconds, but if you can then you have set yourself up with a great video to introduce yourself or your business to a new potential customer. If you are slightly over 15 seconds don't worry too much, but aim to be as close to 15 seconds as you can.

At times you may want to try creating 15-second videos in other formats as well. You can still follow a similar breakdown for other videos. A good general pattern for 15-second videos looks something like this:

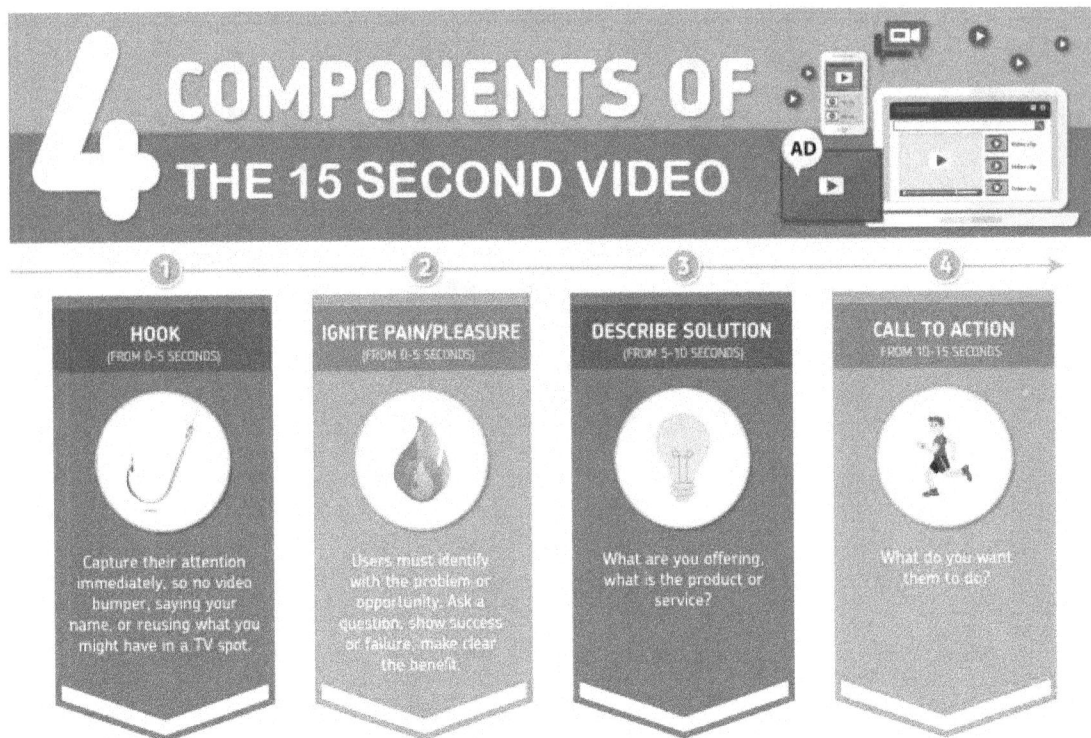

*Image 6.14: 4 Components of 15-Second Videos*

Notice that we still have a hook, highlight a problem/solution, and then include some sort of call to action. You can tweak and adjust this pattern slightly, but this basic breakdown can serve as a formula for you to create powerful 15-second videos. This format works just as well for 30-60 second videos with slightly more time dedicated to each bucket. You can and should test creating videos of different lengths to test in each stage of your funnel.

One key thing to note is that you should never include bumpers at the start of your videos. You only have 2-3 seconds to catch someone's attention and a video that starts with a logo or some other kind of bumper sacrifices crucial time you need to hook your viewer.

## Video Content Creation Tips

One of the great things about TikTok is that the best tool you could have for creating content on the platform is likely sitting within your arm's reach at all times. Video created using your smartphone is perfect for TikTok. You can do some post-filming editing, but remember that authentic-looking content generally outperforms overproduced content on TikTok.

Though smartphone video is perfectly suited, we know that most business owners don't have extensive knowledge or experience creating video content. We've compiled a list of tips and tricks we've learned to help you create high-quality content for your TikTok account.

### Content Organization

- Google Photos app is super slow in uploading your videos from the photos library on your phone. So also pay for iCloud, Dropbox, and Amazon Photos (another $10 each per month) to have your videos automatically backed up. You will have to keep these apps open every week to let them catch up since uploads are faster when the app is open. Using one of these apps will allow your team to access the spontaneous content you are creating without needing to access your phone directly.

- Amazon Photos has the smartest facial recognition and the easiest way to share groups of pictures (instead of having to select each picture/video, one-by-one) with your external parties (like freelancers and partners).

- Only keep the footage you plan on using in order to save time when editing.

- Start by listing out questions that you can answer in one minute. 60 seconds isn't long, so choose topics you can properly cover in that time frame.

- Avoid being too ambitious – break bigger topics into smaller chunks. Your audience prefers to consume many small tidbits versus sitting through a full hour of you talking, especially with the majority of these being consumed on their phones.

- Keep a running list of topics that you would like to cover. As you are going about your day, ideas might pop up so write them down on your phone or somewhere safe so you can keep track of them.

## Additional Content Resources

Though we believe that any business owner can and should create videos for their business, we also understand that you may need some additional help for some situations. In this section, we want to share a few resources we've seen people use to gain some additional help in the content creation process. These resources may cost a bit more than filming with your own smartphone but may be a good match for you and your business.

**Tiktok Creator Marketplace, Cameo, and Billio**
TikTok has a self-hosted marketplace that allows you to recruit content creators to help you create content for your business.

With Open Application Campaigns, brands can list their campaigns for interested creators to self-apply. Once an Open Application Campaign is live, the brand will be able to review the shortlist of creator applications, including relevant metrics and reference videos, to help guide the selection process.

Approved applications can then move forward into partnerships to co-create and amplify campaigns. This feature gives creators more agency to proactively engage with the brands they know and love and allows them to showcase their content creation skills in collaborations. It also deepens the opportunity for brands to discover new creators by democratizing the selection process.

Cameo and Billio are similar platforms that allow you to recruit other public figures or celebrities to talk about your business. You purchase a video and provide feedback on what you would like them to discuss. There are certain guidelines that businesses must follow, but this can be a cool way to generate some high-value content with an easily recognizable face. The figures on these pages range from sports figures to movie stars so you should have no problem finding someone you would be interested in working with.

**TikTok Creative Exchange**
The TikTok Creative Exchange is a self-serve portal that matches you with vetted creative service providers to help produce high-performing ads suited to your brief and objectives. Through this portal, you can manage projects,

feedback, approvals, and insights — all in a streamlined process designed to help you create impactful ads.

The Creative Exchange platform is designed to be a one-stop-shop covering each step of the creative process, all managed through a standardized workflow to enable fast, scalable production and deliver large volumes of fresh creative content. If you have a larger budget and feel like this service could be helpful for your business then this could be a great solution for you to look into.

### Tiktok Instant Page

TikTok Instant Pages are a new feature TikTok released in 2022 for businesses running ads on the platform. These pages are comparable to Facebook's instant articles. Just like FB's articles, Instant Pages load faster for better potential views and conversion.

Businesses can customize these pages in the ads manager with the provided content editor and creation tool, dragging and dropping modules into place.

Besides load time (11x faster than the typical mobile page), these pages offer engaging templates for brands that are looking to create better experiences for their customers. For example, with the build tool, brands can create product carousels and full movie trailers for more engagement and increased reach.

---

## PARETO SUMMARY

---

▷ Customer stories make for some of the best performing TikToks.

▷ You need to embrace the flawsome!

▷ Reuse your best content and turn it into 15-second snippets for TikTok.

▷ Use a content calendar, the Topic Wheel, and spontaneous content for easy TikTok video creation.

▷ We recommend 4 types of content when starting out: 1) why, how, what videos, 2) day in life/behind-the-scenes, 3) testimonials/reviews/case studies, and 4) related news/content curation.

▷ It's about creating a constant stream of TikTok content without spending hours doing it.

▷ People want to be entertained and surprised on TikTok, not blatantly advertised to.

# Chapter Seven:
# Targeting

*Image 7.1: Social Amplification Phases - Targeting*

Targeting on TikTok is a fascinating topic, but this section will be shorter than you might expect. Like other social media platforms, TikTok has demographic, geographic, and interest-based targeting features. It has remarketing audiences and lookalikes that you can use to build your funnel. These are all important, but TikTok has one targeting function that you won't find in your ad settings and which may help protect it from some of the government scrutinies Facebook has faced in recent months.

While Facebook explicitly gives the power to target certain types of people, TikTok really focuses on the content. **The TikTok algorithm uses information from your video to identify your target audience**. Simple things like books in the background can influence where you are shown.

We have seen simple content that hit it big merely because it was filmed at Jake Paul's home. Jake wasn't even in the video, but the algorithm recognized the location and sent that video out to many more people than it would have otherwise reached.

Though Facebook has more targeting features and tells you more explicitly who you are going after, TikTok is arguably more powerful. If you are able to create content that will appeal to your audience and you are able to connect with others in your space, TikTok will do a lot of the heavy lifting of targeting for you. That is why you need to be creating and testing lots of different types of content to find the combination of words, topics, and partners that works for your business.

## How Chirocandy Targets TikToks For Local Chiros:

"Skeptical." That's how Brady Sticker of Chirocandy described his first thoughts of running ads for clients on TikTok.

At that time, Chirocandy was successfully running Facebook Ads for their chiropractor customers.

*TikTok wouldn't be profitable for them*, Brady thought, because Chirocandy was targeting a more mature demographic, adults older than 25.

This "TikTok is for kids" myth is common among businesses and marketers alike, and it's one of the things that has made TikTok one of the best-kept secrets in social media marketing.

It wasn't until one of his clients mentioned to him that they were using another agency for their TikTok ads that Brady decided he needed to start running ads on the platform to make sure he wasn't missing out.

What he found was shocking.

**Chirocandy's TikTok ads converted better than their ads on Facebook.**

Brady and his team found that their TikTok ads had more engagement, cost less, and were more effective at turning leads into actual paying customers for the businesses they served.

For targeting, Brady geo targets as best he can for the 25+ demographic.

Sometimes though he needs to get creative when he wants to market inside a specific region in a designated market area (DMA). Brady gives the example of a chiropractor in the Dallas DMA that wants to target people in a specific suburb.

In this case, he suggests micro-targeting the smaller group by calling them out in the video and then leading them to a form where you can ask them prequalifying questions to figure out where they're located.

Having an offer that resonates with your audience is the main thing, he says, but how well you do can also be dependent on the region you're targeting and how many competitors you have that are also advertising on TikTok.

That's why it's important to get in now, while people are still unaware of the ad potential of TikTok.

I don't know if I want more people to advertise here, Brady says. We're killing it. It's like we're part of a new gold rush.

## TikTok Targeting Options

Though your targeting is heavily influenced by your content, there is still a variety of targeting options you can use within the TikTok advertising platform. Below we've included the official list of targeting options from TikTok in January 2022.

| Audience | Include | • Create a Lookalike or Custom Audience (Customer file, Engagement, App Activity, Website Traffic). |
| --- | --- | --- |
| | Exclude | • Exclude Lookalike or Custom Audiences |
| Demographics | Gender | • Male, Female |
| | Age | • 13-17, 18-24, 25-34, 35-44, 45-54, 55+ |
| | Location | • Deliver to users based on their location: Country/Region, State/Province, Metro Areas, City and US DMA. |
| | Language | • Delivery to users based on app language. |

| Interests and Behaviors | Interests | • Deliver to users based their higher interaction with certain Interests. e.g. "Gaming" |
| --- | --- | --- |
| | Behaviors | • Deliver ads based on user's recent in-app Behavior's such as interactions with videos or creators.<br>• Video behaviors include watching, liking, commenting and sharing videos by category. e.g. "Food", "Fashion".<br>• Creator interactions include following or viewing creator profiles by category. e.g. "Travel", "Sports" |
| Device | Connection Type | • WIFI, 2G, 3G, 4G |
| | Operation System | • iOS & Android |
| | Operation System Version | • Deliver ads to users based on software version. e.g. iOS 10.0 or above. Android 4.0 or above. |
| | Device Model | • Delivery ads to users based on user's device model. |
| | Device Price | • Deliver ads to users based on device pricing, ranging from no limit to $1000+. |
| | Carrier | • Deliver ads to users based on mobile phone carriers. |

*Image 7.2: TikTok Targeting Options Jan 2022*

## TikTok Placements

In addition to the targeting options listed above, you also have the option to select which placements your ads appear on. These placements vary slightly depending on what country you are targeting, but in the US you have the following options:

● TikTok Feed - Ads placed directly in the TikTok feed.

● News Feed Apps - Placed in the feeds of some News app partners of TikTok including BuzzVideo, TopBuzz, News Republic, and Babe.

● Pangle - A video advertising platform focused outside the US.

Our recommendation is to **switch your placement to manual and focus your efforts solely on the TikTok feed**, especially if you are a US-based advertiser. These other apps

may have their place outside of the US, but we generally recommend starting with just the TikTok feed placement.

## PARETO SUMMARY

▷ TikTok has demographic, geographic, and interest-based targeting like other social platforms have.

▷ TikTok has one targeting function you won't find in your ad settings: its algorithm is powerful... **The TikTok algorithm uses information from your video to identify your target audience**. Simple things like books in the background can influence where your videos are shown.

▷ We recommend that you switch to manual placements for your TikTok ads and focus on the TikTok news feed, especially if you're US-based (or targeting US people).

# Chapter Eight:
# Amplification

BUSINESS PACKAGES | 1 PLUMBING | 2 GOALS | 3 CONTENT | 4 TARGETING | 5 AMPLIFICATION | 6 OPTIMIZATION

*Image 8.1: Social Amplification Phases - Amplification*

Now that you have a collection of pieces of content you have posted to your TikTok account, you are prepped and ready to start amplifying your content through paid testing. Sometimes even the best content needs a little boost to get started and this is especially true for your business-focused posts. You are unlikely to go viral with testimonials or other business-focused content, but remember that isn't your goal.

Your goal is to **put small budgets behind your posts to find the winners** so you can then scale your efforts and drive meaningful results for your business. You aren't going to capture everyone's attention, but amplifying your content will help you capture the attention of the people most important to your business.

## TikTok Ad Account Structure

The basic set-up of the TikTok Ads Account is very simple and mirrors Facebook very closely. You start with the campaign where you name your campaign, choose your optimization objective, and make any other campaign-level budget adjustments you would like.

As you are setting this up, remember to think back to the key metrics you selected while setting goals and think about the goal of this particular campaign. Three optimization goals we use most regularly are Video Views, Traffic, and Conversions. We have also seen Lead Generation be useful for individuals looking to use TikTok native lead forms.

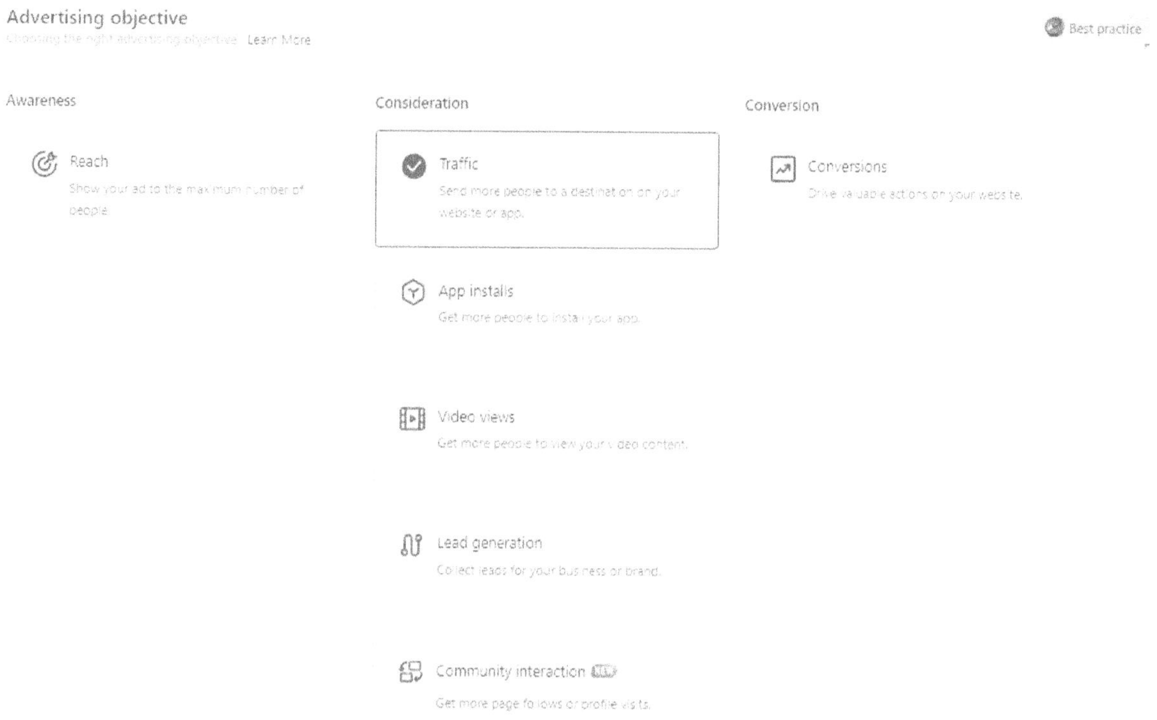

Awareness

Consideration

Conversion

Reach
Show your ad to the maximum number of people

Traffic
Send more people to a destination on your website or app.

Conversions
Drive valuable actions on your website.

App installs
Get more people to install your app.

Video views
Get more people to view your video content.

Lead generation
Collect leads for your business or brand.

Community interaction
Get more page follows or profile visits.

*Image 8.2: TikTok Ad Setup*

Once you've completed your campaign set-up you are taken to the Ad Group section. Here you set your budget (TikTok currently requires a minimum of $20 a day), set your targeting and location, choose your placements, and further refine your optimization goals. If you are optimizing for conversions, this means you will specifically be choosing which conversion event you are optimizing for.

If you are a US-based advertiser we strongly recommend only utilizing the TikTok Ads placement. To do this you will need to switch off automatic placements and choose select placements.

Placements

Placement type

Automatic placement
Automatically show your ads across supported placements. Learn more

◉ Select placement
Manually choose your targeting placement. Learn more

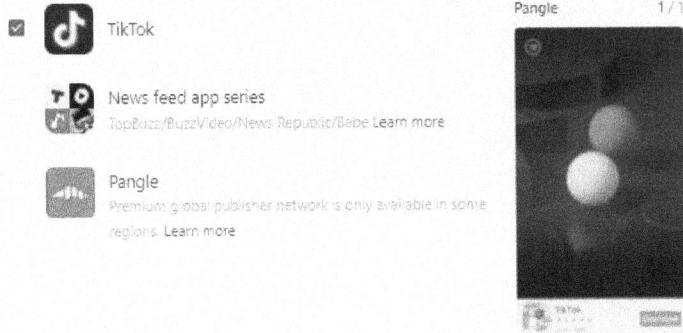

☑ ♪ TikTok

News feed app series
TopBuzz/BuzzVideo/News Republic/Babe Learn more

Pangle
Premium global publisher network is only available in some
regions. Learn more

Pangle                                    1 / 1

*Image 8.3: TikTok Ad Placement Options*

In the ads section of the account structure, you will be able to upload
videos, ad text, and choose your destination URL. In this section, you can
also utilize the native TikTok video editor to add text overlays and other
enhancements to your videos. The ads you create here will not be shown on
your TikTok account, but you can upload a logo and username you would
like to use for your ads at this stage.

As you add pieces to your ad you will see the preview on the right side of
your screen update so you can double-check everything looks and sounds
like you would like it to.

## TikTok Ad Considerations

● You want to set the campaign budget to "no limit" by default. If you
uncheck it, the budget must be at least $50 a day to continue, no matter
what objective.

Budget

No limit

Daily              5.00                                    USD

Your budget must be a number between 50.00 and 10,000,000.00.

*Image 8.4: TikTok Ad Budget Options*

This is not practically a concern, since we control budgets at the ad group level (which is $20/day minimum).

● If you're running multiple ad groups, then you could activate Campaign Budget Optimization (CBO) to allow TikTok to allocate spend between ad groups, just like Facebook does.

● If you are targeting more than one country, split them into separate campaigns:

● Our account is only allowed to target these countries (8 shown here plus Canada-- so 9 total):

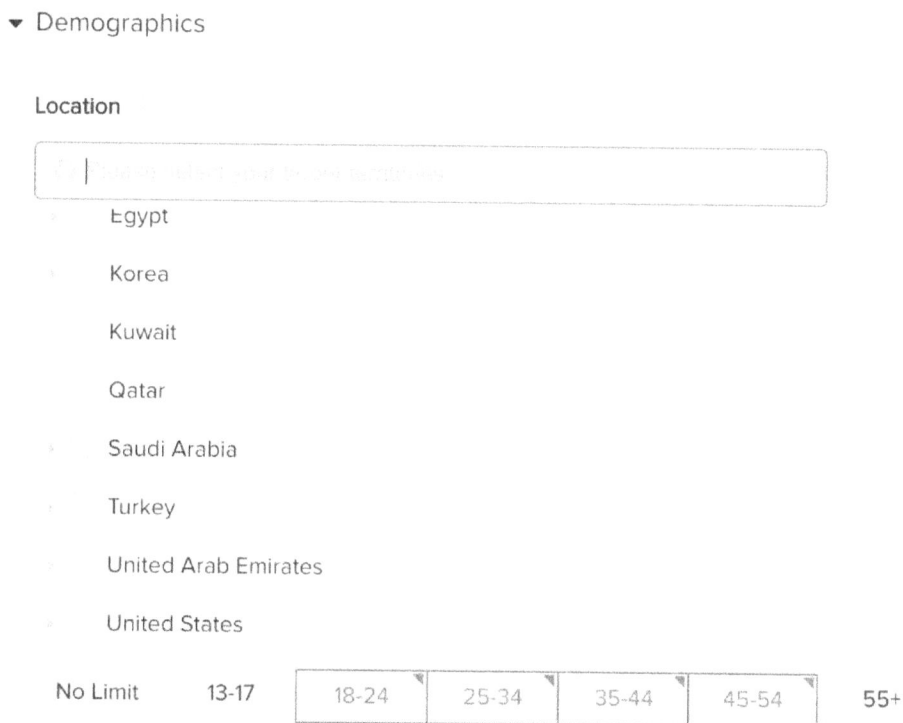

▼ Demographics

Location

Egypt

Korea

Kuwait

Qatar

Saudi Arabia

Turkey

United Arab Emirates

United States

| No Limit | 13-17 | 18-24 | 25-34 | 35-44 | 45-54 | 55+ |

*Image 8.5: TikTok Ad Country Targeting Options*

Many international friends are not able to target the United States, so you need to either have an ad account in the country you're targeting or get an exception from TikTok ad support.

● Important: do not keep budgets running continuously at the ad group level. Otherwise, the ad groups could potentially run out of control if you forget to check on them. We like to let ad groups run for a week, similar to the "Dollar a Day" strategy:

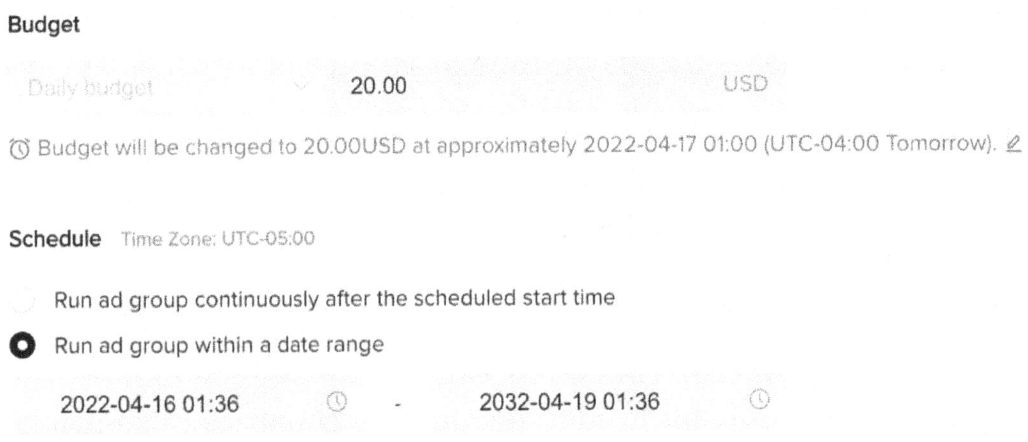

**Budget**

| | | |
|---|---|---|
| Daily budget | 20.00 | USD |

🕐 Budget will be changed to 20.00USD at approximately 2022-04-17 01:00 (UTC-04:00 Tomorrow). ✎

**Schedule**  Time Zone: UTC-05:00

○  Run ad group continuously after the scheduled start time

●  Run ad group within a date range

2022-04-16 01:36  🕐   -   2032-04-19 01:36  🕐

*Image 8.6: TikTok Ad Group Budget Date Range*

● When running a Spark Ad, whether boosting someone else's post or our own, it's most effective to boost positive mentions from clients, partners, employees, and creators. Simply enter the authorization code they give you for that particular post:

**Apply for authorization**                                                                  ✕

Enter TikTok post code and preview the post

| ⊦TvB+VuwQ6hLLToixC+EjFqlW7BjR+OhJTQQ+NTk3CFHxbryaGr1OS/M1nlukz1by7Q | Search |
|---|---|

*Image 8.7: TikTok Spark Ads - Authorization Post Code*

And their post will show up:

Enter TikTok post code and preview the post

#vHwQFYuaP1OFv+TvB+VuwQ6hLLToixC+EjFqlW7BjR+OhJTQQ+NTk3CFHxbryaGr | Search

Preview

Lucas Kalango | Marketing
221935594007138304

Falando sobre TikTok, Crescimento, Algoritmo de TikTok Ads no podcast do fera do marketing e Ads @dennisyu5 (em breve o episódio será publicado e posto aqui 😵) #podcast #tiktokbrasil #aprendanotiktok #tiktokparanegocios #comocrescernotiktok #algoritmo #tiktokads

| Duration | Resolution | Size | Bitrate |
|----------|------------|------|---------|
| 41 s | 720x1280 | 18 MB | 3.70 Mbps |

*Image 8.8: Spark Ad Authorization Accepted*

You do have to select the post again below to be able to continue, perhaps if you're wanting to promote multiple posts (from one or multiple accounts).

## The Importance of Spark Ads

If you've ever boosted a post on Facebook, Spark Ads use a similar method in promoting your posts. Promoting your posts in this way takes the TikTok video posted to your account and promotes it exactly as it is. This works really well for posts that don't require a clear call to action such as why or how videos, content curation posts, or engagement-focused ads.

These ads are also really great if you are working with other content creators or public figures on TikTok as you can put spend in your ad account behind posts they have made on their page.

There is one overwhelming reason, however, why you should use Spark Ads as often as you can. When you create a Spark Ad, both your organic and paid engagement stats will be

combined, drastically increasing the social proof on any given video you have created.

This is a huge benefit and can help you build videos with massive engagement and view counts with no separation between paid and organic views. The social proof you can generate with Spark Ads is impressive and can be a huge game-changer for your business.

**Creating a Spark Ad**

This promotion method has two paths you can take to create these ads.

As mentioned above, the first method uses something called a video code, which essentially acts as an approval key, verifying that you have received authorization from the owner of the video to promote that post for a set period of time. Currently, TikTok allows those video codes to remain active for 7, 30, or 60 days so if you are using this method, you will have to keep that in mind. Make sure you paste that code into a word document or note as you will need it later.

After generating that video code, you can create a campaign and ad group as normal, but once you reach the ad stage your process changes slightly. At the top of the screen where you would normally set your identity, you should see an option to toggle on the Use TikTok account to deliver Spark Ads. If you switch that on, you will be given two new options. If using a spark code, you want to select "Use other authorized account or post."

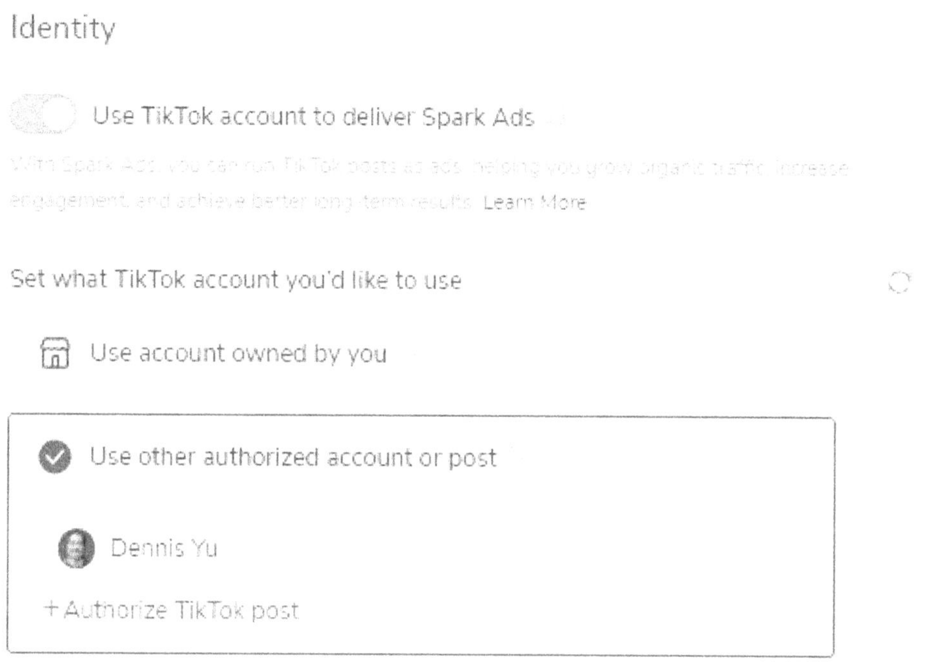

Identity

Use TikTok account to deliver Spark Ads

With Spark Ads, you can run TikTok posts as ads, helping you grow organic traffic, increase engagement, and achieve better long-term results. Learn More

Set what TikTok account you'd like to use

Use account owned by you

Use other authorized account or post

Dennis Yu

+ Authorize TikTok post

*Image 8.9: Spark Ad Setup*

This will give you the option to click to *Authorize TikTok Post*. When you click on that text, you will be presented with a box where you can paste your Spark code and authorize the post.

The second method can be seen just above this Video Code method listed as "Use account owned by you." If you select that option you will be given the power to link a single TikTok account to your TikTok Ad Account.

If you click on Link Account, you will be taken to a login screen where you can login to your business's TikTok profile and link it to your ad account.

For now, this can only be done with one TikTok account, so make sure you only use this method for your most commonly used TikTok account and not for other creators you may be partnering with. This will save you time as you won't have to generate a video code for each ad you want to make *and* there is no expiration date on those promo windows.

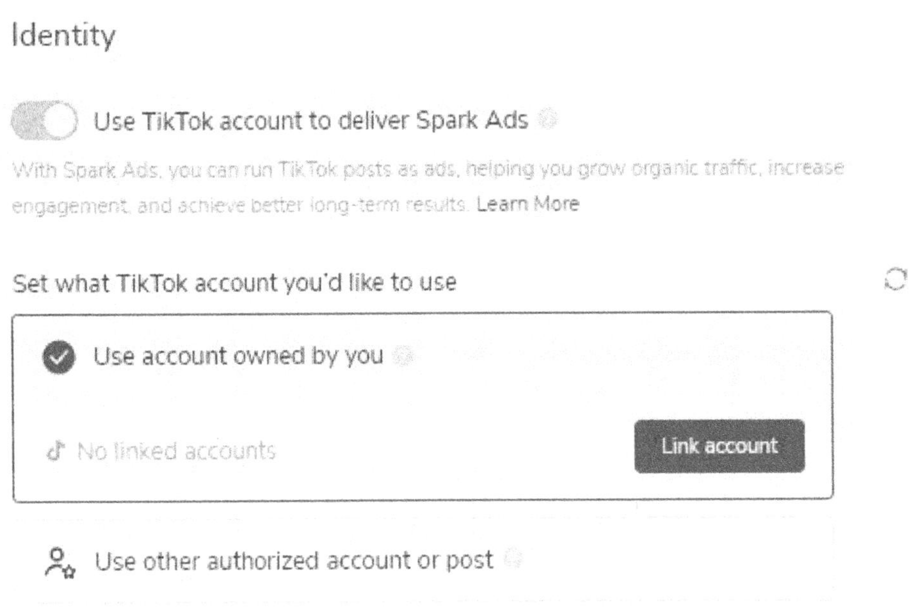

Identity

Use TikTok account to deliver Spark Ads

With Spark Ads, you can run TikTok posts as ads, helping you grow organic traffic, increase engagement, and achieve better long-term results. Learn More

Set what TikTok account you'd like to use

> Use account owned by you

> No linked accounts                    **Link account**

Use other authorized account or post

*Image 8.10: Choosing TikTok Account For Spark Ad*

## PARETO SUMMARY

▷ We start off with organic posts then turn them into ads once we've confirmed they are winners.

▷ TikTok ad campaigns are similar in setup to a Facebook ad.

▷ Spark Ads are excellent for collaboration and posts that don't need clear CTAs.

# Chapter Nine:
# 80/20 Traffic Using TikTok Ads

When you do publicity like writing books or magazine articles or blogging, the publicity itself will almost never close the deal for you. It will just move you to the front of the line. But you still have to get in the line (Or better yet, make *them* get in *your* line).

At a minimum, you need a mechanism for turning the publicity into a sales funnel, like an offer of a diagnostic tool or problem-solving cheat sheet.

You can say, *"Enter your email and we'll send you the cheat sheet."* Then there needs to be a next step and a next step after that. A conveyor belt that moves everything forward.

And in order to get that conveyor belt moving, you need traffic. And while there's a huge range of media outlets you can use to get in front of people and/or acquire customers, you can't effectively be everywhere all at once.

## The Yin and Yang of Media and Traffic Expertise

The yin: It's impossible to become proficient in every form of advertising. You need to focus on one to three forms of marketing and advertising and become more skilled than most people in the use of those media.

The yang: If your entire business is dependent upon one source of traffic, one advertising medium, your business is a stool with only one leg. A train wreck waiting to happen. You need to get new customers from a diverse range of sources.

Chances are if you're reading this book, you've already used Facebook, Google, or other ad platforms effectively in your marketing and advertising.

Now it's time to diversify further. And the opportunity right now lies with mobile-first platforms like TikTok.[3]

When using social media to drive traffic to your business, whether paid or not, it's important to understand that social media platforms are an amplifier of what's already working for your business.

What channels are already working for you?

What creatives and what audiences are working for your business right now? Is it a sales campaign or a PPC (pay-per-click) ad? Is there a webinar that has brought a lot of traffic to your site or brought you lots of conversions?

You want to take the most effective parts of these marketing campaigns, extract video components from them and create short videos that are in line with the three stages of the funnel:

- **Awareness:** Why does your business exist? What is the reason you're doing what you're doing?
- **Consideration:** How do you manifest this "Why" in the world? What are the different skills and techniques you use that qualify to achieve this purpose?
- **Conversion:** What is your product?

By leveraging what's already working, you're not only saving time and money, but you're ensuring better conversions because you're using your greatest hits from other platforms to feed Tiktoks's algorithm.

As a local business, doesn't it make sense to optimize your time and only focus on a platform that is going to bring you the most targeted results?

Especially when you're looking to 80/20 your efforts.

Social media advertising is less about advertising and more about paid word of mouth. Third-party authority mentions and reviews convert better because they generate implied endorsement. Something that the TikTok platform does better than any other social media outlet at the time of writing this book.

And when you utilize the most popular mobile social networking apps in your business, you're able to 80/20 your focus. And that's where TikTok ads come into the mix.

TikTok is the fastest-growing mobile social networking app[4], and it's entirely focused on short video content.

If you want to truly **build the know, like, and trust factor** with your audience, one of the best ways to do this is through video. Something you've likely experienced if you've been using Facebook and Instagram stories, lives, reels, etc. already.

That's why TikTok ads are so powerful (and so easy to do!).

**Moving from Facebook to TikTok**
Before social media, advertisers online were much more product-focused. They were able to rigorously test headlines, ad copy, and images and iterate to fit the needs and preferences of their customers.

With Facebook, advertising became much more focused on the person producing the ad. Personal branding and building relationships with the buyer were much more important.

There was also a big focus on producing large amounts of content. Instead of testing ads, the volume of content produced and the metrics that Facebook provided allowed us to pick winners and amplify them as long as they continued to get interaction.

With TikTok, advertising is much more about the event, the story. It's no longer the product that is in view or the person, but what's happening at the moment. These moments need to be fast and short, 15-second videos that are lightweight and can readily capture attention.

**Like Facebook, with TikTok, the more ads you put out the better you begin to understand your audience and the more of a chance you'll create an ad that qualifies as a win.** Because they're only 15 seconds, you can create tons of these within a small amount of time each day and begin to see great results.

TikTok is all about short videos built on an endless scrolling feed. Its algorithm is distinct from other media platforms in that it is entirely focused on the signal of video engagement.

The algorithm's main goal is to get users to continue to interact on TikTok and so it tracks the patterns of user behavior in order to serve up more relevant videos that will increase their time on the site.

One of the great things about using such a smart algorithm like this is that we don't have to target our audience. The algorithm does it for us. What's more important here is to create content that resonates with and commands the attention of your audience.

The more you can do that, the better your ads will perform.

**A word of caution**
Before you dive into TikTok ads though, may I offer a word of caution...

**TikTok ads work best in an existing business**. It will help increase your conversion rates and gain more of your ideal customer.

It's not for unproven products or businesses that don't have an existing funnel.

You'll do well to start with Facebook first, and as Perry says in his book, *80/20 Sales and Marketing*, "Most direct- and online-marketing success stories I've seen over the last 10 years have this in common: The entrepreneur became extremely proficient at the use of ONE sales channel and used it to develop a firm foothold in a desperately competitive marketplace."

Even though Facebook is problematic right now due to ongoing privacy restrictions with companies like Apple, Facebook is still a good place to start.

For example, Facebook claims the recent changes Apple has made to the way their users can be tracked has cost them $10 billion. The loss of data from users rejecting "the prompt" to allow tracking and Facebook's own removal of detailed targeting puts more burden on the content itself.

Thus, the most successful Facebook advertisers are running conversion campaigns on broad targeting using dynamic ads – letting the algorithm do the targeting and optimization from your contents performance and data we pass back.

Setting up the same tracking, as we covered in the meaty chapter on Digital Plumbing (Chapter Five), allows us to tap into TikTok's equally, if not more powerful optimization algorithm.

TikTok has far fewer targeting options than Facebook, demands higher video quality than Facebook, and has more 30+ (aged) users right now. The 30+ demographic is growing faster, as is typical of social networks that age up. In 8-10 years, there will likely be another social network that is like Facebook is to TikTok right now... And that yet-to-be-invented social network will be the hot new thing. And so the cycle will repeat.

And while we expect users to migrate to TikTok (more for entertainment, while keeping Facebook for friends' updates), we're going to run ads on both platforms.

To be clear: We are not decrying the death of Facebook.

Ready to get started?

## Organic Engagement

Though this book is ostensibly about ads, the viral component of organic is a signal for paid. Right now, the purely organic strategy does generate more traffic overall. But going viral is "hit and miss," as has always been the case with the early days of new platforms.

Eventually, organic dwindles and ads become the steady way to scale since we can't grow if we're not in alignment with the platform's objectives.

For the 5% of the people who are good enough on video to do well organically -- or are in a hot area, they can rely on organic methods alone.

For the rest of us who are business owners, perhaps in non-sexy industries, we *can* rely on ads.

Consider the following:

> • **Posts from personal Tik Tok accounts do get more traction** -- not because business accounts are limited, but since personal accounts are allowed to do duets and use copyrighted material. We know viral sounds

are key to a lot of growth, but business accounts can run ads and get proper analytics.

• **Do hashtags still work on TikTok?** Yes, but they will gradually lose effectiveness. Use them but use them wisely. For example, we used to be able to add #fyp to get more placement on the "for you" page, but this doesn't work anymore. Because TikTok is algorithmically-driven by content virality, not by search or your friends' activity, more hashtags could serve to water down the post. Plus, the caption is less noticed compared to Instagram and Facebook.

• **Will the pricing of TikTok ads eventually catch up with Facebook?** Yes. When Instagram first launched as a special placement, ad load was low, so average CPMs were 50 cents. But as advertisers started to make 15-second vertical videos and Facebook enabled "all placements" as a default setting, there were more ads competing for the inventory. Now, as of early 2022, average CPMs are over $12 on Facebook. We expect this traffic arbitrage opportunity on TikTok to last another 24-36 months.

Once you've got your content pieces identified and you have some videos ready, then you'll want to set up your TikTok Ads account.

---

## PARETO SUMMARY

▷ When it comes to traffic + TikTok, it's about identifying what is already working on your other channels and transferring that over to TikTok.

▷ Social media advertising is less about advertising and more about paid word of mouth.

▷ If you want to truly **build the know, like, and trust factor** with your audience, one of the best ways to do this is through video.

▷ You don't need to sing and dance on TikTok to be effective.

▷ TikTok ads are not for unproven products or businesses that don't have an existing funnel.

▷ Organic content dwindles and ads become the steady way to scale.

# Chapter Ten:
# Making Your TikTok Campaigns Fly:
# The Magic of a Website that Does Its Job Well

In 1903, at the same time that Orville and Wilbur Wright were struggling to fly the world's first airplane at Kitty Hawk, North Carolina, another inventor, Samuel Pierpont Langley, was also trying to build an airplane – with the assistance of an entire staff.

Langley's assumption was that if he put a big enough engine on the airplane, it would fly. He focused all his effort on that one project: creating a powerful engine for the plane.

The Wright Brothers' approach, however, was to build a glider that would glide from a hilltop with no engine at all. They focused their energy on balance and steering – power was almost an afterthought. Only after it worked with no power would they try to put an engine on it.

After three years of tedious experimentation, the glider was working well, so they commissioned bicycle shop machinist Charlie Taylor to build them an engine. It was the smallest engine he could design – a twelve-horsepower unit that weighed 180 pounds.

Meanwhile, Langley built a much larger engine, mounted it on his airplane, and called a press conference. Rudyard Kipling tells the tragic story:

*I met Professor Langley of the Smithsonian, an old man who had designed a model airplane driven—for petrol had not yet arrived—by a miniature flash-boiler engine, a marvel of delicate craftsmanship. It flew on trial over two hundred yards and drowned itself in the waters of the Potomac, which was the cause of great mirth and humor to the Press of his country.*

*The plane crashed immediately after leaving the launch pad, badly damaging the front wing.*

*Two months later, just eight days before the Wright brothers' successful flight, Langley made a second attempt. This time the tail and rear wing collapsed completely during launch.*

*Langley was ridiculed by the press and criticized by members of Congress for throwing away taxpayer dollars on his failed projects. (Can you imagine the cynicism? I'm sure many sneering reporters believed that nobody could or would ever fly.) Disillusioned by the public response, Langley abandoned his vision.*

Needless to say, the Wright Brothers transformed the world and became famous historical figures, while few have ever heard of Mr. Langley. Their approach of making the plane fly before applying high power was the superior one.

> *"Langley had spent most of four years building an extraordinary engine to lift their heavy flying machine. The Wrights had spent most of four years building a flying machine so artfully designed that it could be propelled into the air by a fairly ordinary internal combustion engine." –* Smithsonian Magazine, April 2003

The world's first manned flight is a direct analogy to your success on TikTok.

**TikTok advertising is the engine. Your website is the glider.** A motor without a good set of wings does you no good. But when you put an engine on a workable glider, you have a plane; when you feed traffic to a website that can "fly," you have a business.

If you have an effective website that simply lacks traffic, you have a glider; just put a lightweight engine on it and you'll fly. But if you have traffic that's going to a lousy website, you don't have a business. You have a money pit.

**Here's the lesson**:

TikTok can bring you a lot of traffic, but it's only valuable to the extent that your website is designed to convert the traffic to leads and sales.

Again, it's about visitor value. You grow it by having a quality website.

So as you're getting started, TikTok ads are like a lightweight engine that you can turn on and off instantly. You can test your glider safely without crashing, killing a potential joint venture partnership, or burning through a lot of cash.

## The Unlimited Traffic Technique

I learned this from Jonathan Mizel, a reclusive mass consumer marketer who occasionally emerges from his cave in Maui, Hawaii, to teach a seminar or release a training course. He's a genius. Jonathan says that when you can convert a visitor to a dollar better than everyone else in your niche, you can buy their traffic from them because they'll make more money selling their visitors to you than they make by keeping the visitors to themselves.

This means that the most important thing you ever do is grow your Value Per Visitor. How do you do that? You test videos and landing pages.

**The Unlimited Traffic Technique** - testing until you have the best Value Per Visitor and then scaling up and out - will become extremely important in chapters [Chapter 7 about scaling up and Chapter 8 warning about diversification] because once your sales funnel and website convert well on TikTok, you've achieved the first step to making it convert on other platforms. This protects you from the world's most dangerous number: ONE.

One traffic source, one product, one employee, all your eggs in one basket...

---

### PARETO SUMMARY

---

▷ TikTok advertising is the engine. Your website is the glider. A motor without a good set of wings does you no good. But when you put an engine on a workable glider, you have a plane; when you feed traffic to a website that can "fly," you have a business.

▷ The most important thing you ever do is grow your Value Per Visitor. How do you do that? You test videos and landing pages using The Unlimited Traffic Technique.

# Chapter Eleven:
# 80/20 Scaling-up Massively

Once you've tested and done your homework—once you're scratching the right itches, once you're converting people at a healthy rate, you can massively expand your business.

## 80/20 for Ads

Carlos Garcia is a maverick banner ad buyer. I once asked him, "What's the secret of banner ads?"

His reply: *"Test 50 ads. One of them's going to be a crazy winner."*

You write 50 ads. Eventually, one of them's gonna fetch as much traffic as the other 49 put together. The good news is that most people don't even test five. That's the 80/20 of ad writing, and in online advertising, testing is what separates the men from the boys, the women from the girls...

## Optimizing TikTok Ads

*Image 11.1: Social Amplification Phases - Optimization*

How do you know if your video is performing? By checking your statistics against these benchmarks:

● Reach - this will vary based on the target audiences you've chosen
● Views - ideally this should equate to 50% of your total reach. So for every 1,000 reach, you'd want 500 views
● View Length:
    ○ Less than 3 seconds - poor
    ○ 6 seconds - average
    ○ 10 seconds - good
    ○ 15-20 seconds - great
    ○ 30+ seconds - you're a Unicorn!

From there, we like to optimize further. We want to see views turn into 10-second views as follows:

- Less than 30% watch the first 10 seconds - poor/average
- 20-40% watch the first 10 seconds - good
- 50% watch the first 10 seconds - great

**Pareto Point**

We're focused on producing and optimizing 15-second videos, so we want to look at completion rates. If we are over 20%, we've got a winner.

The longer the video, the lower the completion rate. So that's why we are making it so short.

## Increase Your Sales 50 Times in 4 Steps

Let's say your best performing TikTok videos are getting 10-15 second views, which is good from our video benchmarking from the Conversions chapter. This is your starting point.

Here's what you do next:

1. Turn up the budget for the campaign,
2. Expand the audience,
3. Raise the CPA target (because they increase the LTV), and
4. Try to beat the existing creative.

**Pareto Point**

Just like on Facebook, instead of trying to promote 50 random things in 50 random ways—keep honing the one thing that's performed the best.

As mentioned in chapter 8, where we talk in-depth about The Content Factory, another part of scaling up TikTok ads is harnessing the positive feedback of clients/customers—so that what they say becomes the TikToks we put dollars against.

## TikTok Optimization With Padfield Media

What makes a successful TikTok ad? *The ad creative is 90% of the process and the other 10% is figuring out how to position a brand so it looks native to the platform*, says Eliot Padfield of Padfield Media.

Eliot is an 18-year-old wunderkind that has become a giant in the TikTok ad space. His media company, based in Los Angeles, focuses on helping fortune 500 companies succeed at making ads for the TikTok ecosystem.

Frequently you can find him on Twitter posting tweets about how companies can improve their TikTok conversions.

Eliot sees TikTok as nothing short of revolutionary. **Unlike other social media platforms where ads look like ads, what does really well on TikTok are ads that look like everything else on the platform.**

The goal is to blend within the community you're trying to target and engage and entertain them. For this reason, Eliot says, you don't need the harsh CTA like on other platforms.

The approach is more relational, and often it takes more touches with your audience than it does on Facebook to get a conversion, but with the low cost of ads, it still makes sense to use this platform.

Brands need to follow the trends, look like they're native to the platform, and also have a distinct personality that their community loves to interact with.

That's why when looking at metrics that point to a successful ad, Padfield Media looks at both the quantitative data coming in, like ROAS, but also focuses heavily on the qualitative data, to get a bigger picture of the effect the ad has on the community.

Eliot argues that it is this qualitative data that helps a brand see how people are reacting, and allows brands to foresee trends and consumer sentiment. We can use this qualitative data as a lens to better discern your other metrics.

TikTok is incredibly individualistic. An ad is never going to be perfect for every single one of a brand's target customers. **The TikTok demographic**

**is largely one that values trust, and trust takes time**.

It's not about the creators. It's about the consumers. That's why brands need to continually iterate and run ads at a huge scale to learn how to adapt and make content that their customers genuinely like to consume.

## Metrics > Analysis > Action

This section will help you understand the basics of a framework called #MAA (Metrics > Analysis > Action) in conjunction with #CID (Communicate > Iterate > Delegate).

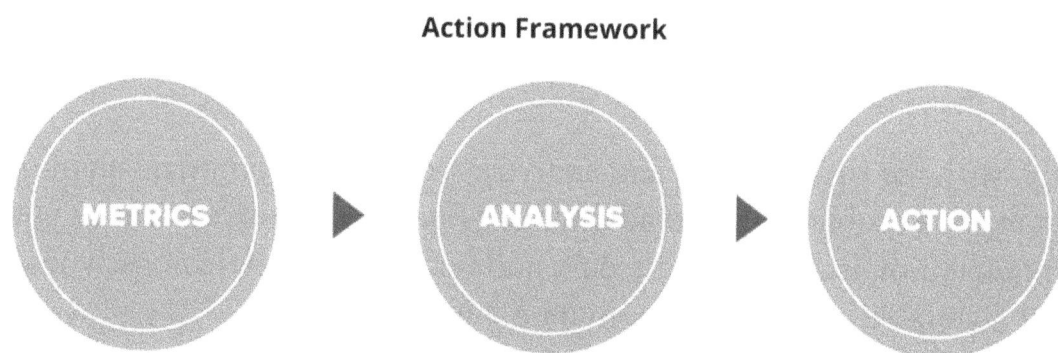

*Image 11.3: #MMA Framework*

Before we can start using the #MAA Framework, you'll need to ensure you've installed the TikTok Pixel and you'll want to ensure that you've set up conversion tracking correctly in your Google Analytics account with TikTok as a source. We covered that in Chapter Four.

In optimization (to help us with conversion), you're using data to answer these questions:

- How are my different marketing channels performing relative to one another, and where am I bleeding?

- What is the right amount of effort and spend to place on Pay Per Click, email marketing, Search Engine Optimization, offline campaigns, and social media?

- How much provable profit, Return on Investment, and margin are being generated by each of my marketing campaigns?

- Based on the data, what are the top 10 specific things that my organization can do to improve metrics?

## Optimization Framework: #MAA

Optimization cannot happen without the right data. To find the right data, first, you need to know your business marketing goals. This means the (1) desired action and (2) its value to the business. These two pieces of information combined will enable you to align optimization efforts with your business's goals.

Once you have the right metrics, you have to make sense of it. Metrics without analysis are just numbers. They do not mean anything to the business. The goal of analysis is to answer the question, "so what?" Analysis helps you identify the (1) root problem or (2) present opportunity. Either of these is always present.

Finally, with the right metrics and analysis, you will recommend a course of action to fix a problem or take advantage of an opportunity. Because your recommendation is supported by data and reasonable conclusions, you can present a suitable solution and convince others.

This 3-step process is called #MAA - M for metrics, and AA for Analysis and Action.

## METRICS

Starting from your most important metrics, clearly display trends. By placing your metrics in context to be more meaningful, cost per acquisition is counterbalanced by the number of conversions, click-through rate is balanced by average position, the conversion rate is balanced by cost per click, and so forth. By balancing your metrics, you can avoid making a decision that helps us in one area while accidentally hurting us in another.

## ANALYSIS

By systematically choosing pairs of derived metrics in the pyramid, we can drill down into the root causes of WHY a metric may have changed. Not just knowing that revenue per customer is up, but understanding the underlying reasons why - a different campaign mix, the addition of a large customer that swings the average, seasonality, a large email blast, and so forth. Avoid the lie of averages. Set up alerts to spot problems before they get out of control.

## ACTION

Now that you know why a particular metric changed, take one of the multiple recommended actions to correct a problem. You can set up your own expert system rules and conduct experiments on landing pages, navigation, pricing models, and so forth. This is closed-loop marketing.

Before you can apply the #MAA Framework, let's figure out what we need to pay attention to.

## Top N

Top N is a sorting technique that helps you prioritize things to pay attention to. It applies not just to digital marketing campaigns. Whether you know it or not, we apply Top N every day.

When we wake up, we choose to brush our teeth before eating breakfast. We choose to watch Netflix, play football, and do homework (hopefully) before we go to bed. We make choices among a sea of other things that we could have done. That is the essence of Top N.

When it comes to running digital marketing campaigns, we often have tens of campaigns, hundreds of ad sets, and thousands of ads all running at the same time. We cannot possibly pay attention to everything, hence the need to prioritize.

Therein begs the question, *"which campaigns/ad sets/ads should I look at?"* Fortunately, there are only a few important dimensions we usually have to consider: ad spend, cost per action, and the number of actions.

The top 5-10 ad sets by ad spend often account for the majority (more than 50%) of total spend. Compare that to spending hours optimizing 100 ad sets. The effort you put into the top 5-10 would have made a similar impact to optimizing the other 90-95 ad sets.

Similarly, sorting ad sets by cost per action reveals the most expensive ads that are wasting money. If the conditions of statistical significance are met, killing off these ads will take no more than five minutes.

But optimization is not about getting cheaper cost per action. It is about achieving as many goals as possible within constraints, like cost per action. This principle applies no matter what stage of the funnel you are currently working in. You could be trying to generate as many video views as you can at the top of your funnel, provided you are only paying $.02 per view or you could be trying to drive as many purchases as possible while maintaining your profit margin.

Looking at just the top 5-10 ad sets by a number of actions, you may see opportunities to scale and get even more. As long as the cost of each action falls within the cost constraint (i.e., each action is profitable), it makes sense to spend more, create more content, or expand the same content to reach more people.

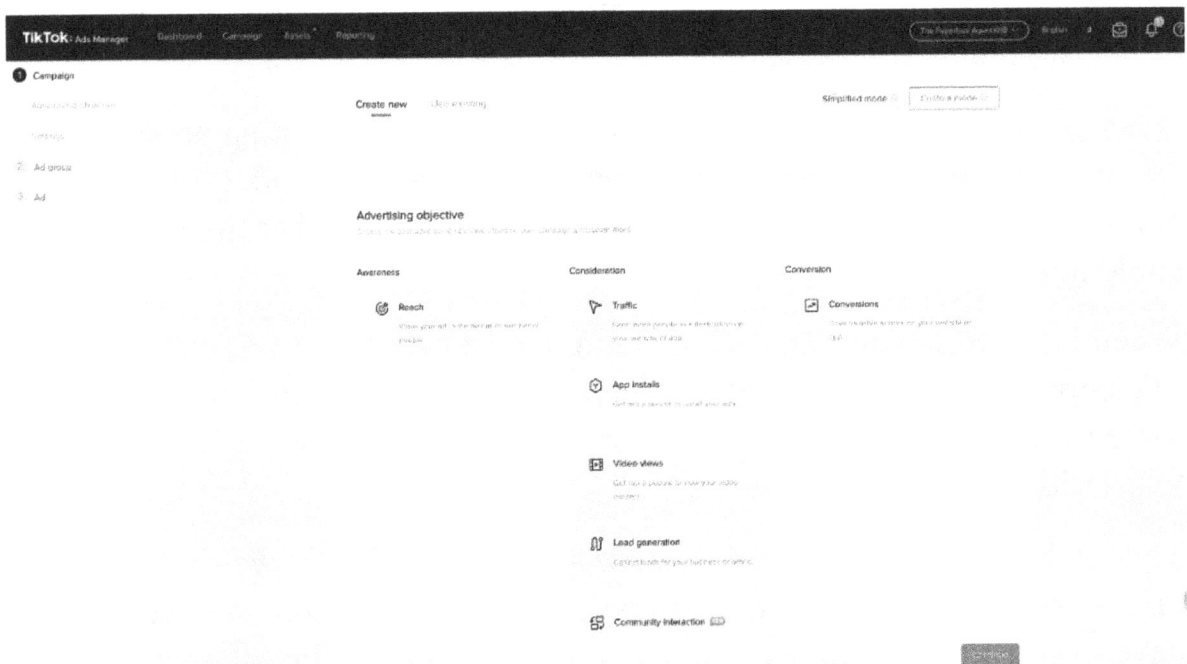

*Image 11.4: Account Campaign Structure For Campaign Creation*

Watch this video for a breakdown of this concept:
https://tinyurl.com/topnsorting

### Metrics Decomposition
So how do you move from metrics to analysis? The answer is in Metrics Decomposition.

A seemingly complex concept, Metrics Decomposition describes the relationship between many different metrics. This relationship enables you to make sense of changes in results, like a sudden change in cost per action or a spike in conversions. It keeps you calm because you will be able to figure out what went wrong/right.

- This is the profit formula behind Facebook ads – not sales puffery, but a mathematically derived formula.

- It starts with applying the conventional profit formula: Profits = Revenue - Cost.

- Revenue from TikTok = Value per conversion x No. of conversions. If an apple costs $5 and you sell 5 apples on TikTok, your revenue is $5 x 5 = $25.

- Cost from TikTok = No. of conversions x Cost per conversion. If you spent $3 to sell an apple, your cost is $3 x 5 = $15.

- Your profit is thus $25 - $15 = $10.

Unfortunately, this is where many beginner marketing consultants stop. Let's say, today, you sell 5 apples at $5 each, so you don't make a profit. How would you go about finding out what the problem is?

**Here's how we would do it**:

- Compare the conversion rates today versus yesterday. Did fewer people buy per 100 visitors?

- If not, compare the visits on both days. Did fewer people come along?

- This or the previous point must be true.

- If conversion rates stayed the same, but visits dropped, compare click-through rates on both days. Did fewer people click on my ad per every 100 impressions?

- Otherwise, compare the number of impressions served. Were there fewer impressions?

We could go on and on for the next few paragraphs, but you get the point.

## Troubleshooting Conversions

Your profit is a function of cost and revenue, maximized where marginal revenue equals marginal cost. A bit of first-semester economics will help you find the spend level that maximizes profit, which is not the same as maximizing margin or revenue.

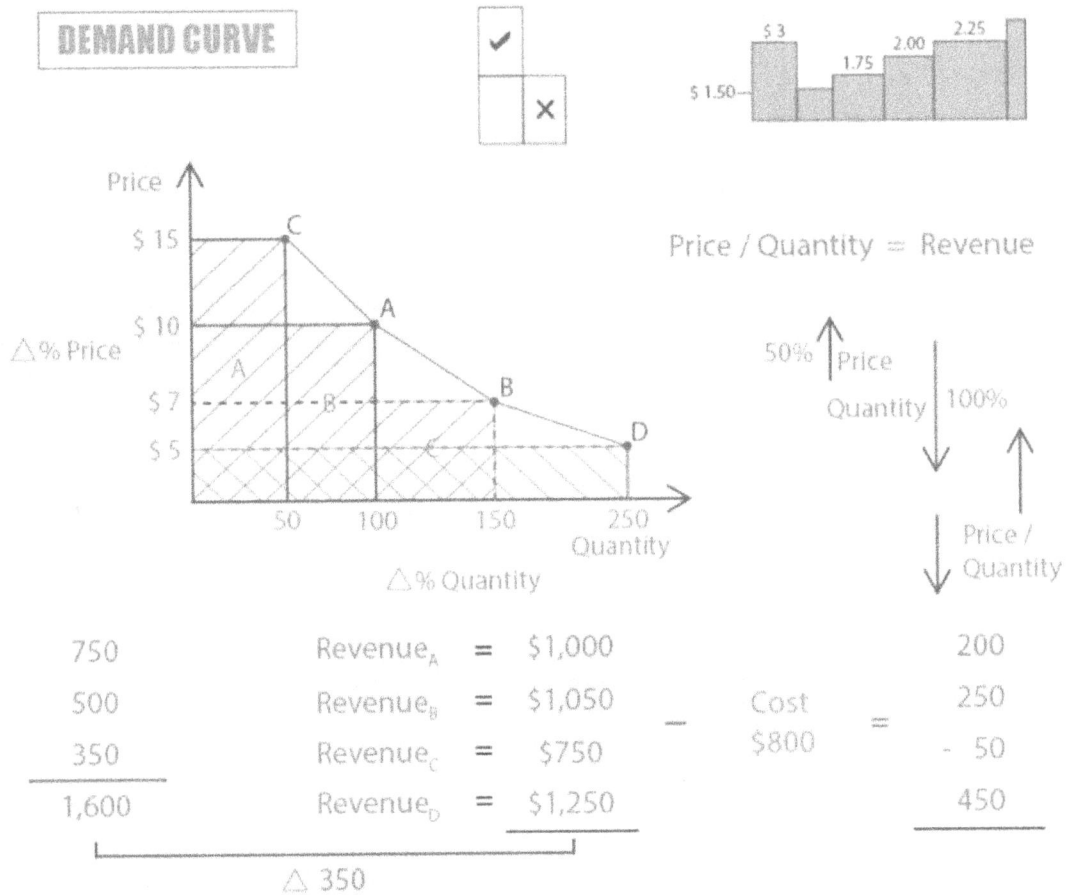

*Image 11.5: Troubleshooting Conversions*

## Step-By-Step Checklist

### APPLY TOP N
*Step 1.*
Select campaigns by stage (Awareness, Consideration, Conversion). View campaigns at the ad set level. Sort ad sets by amount spent.

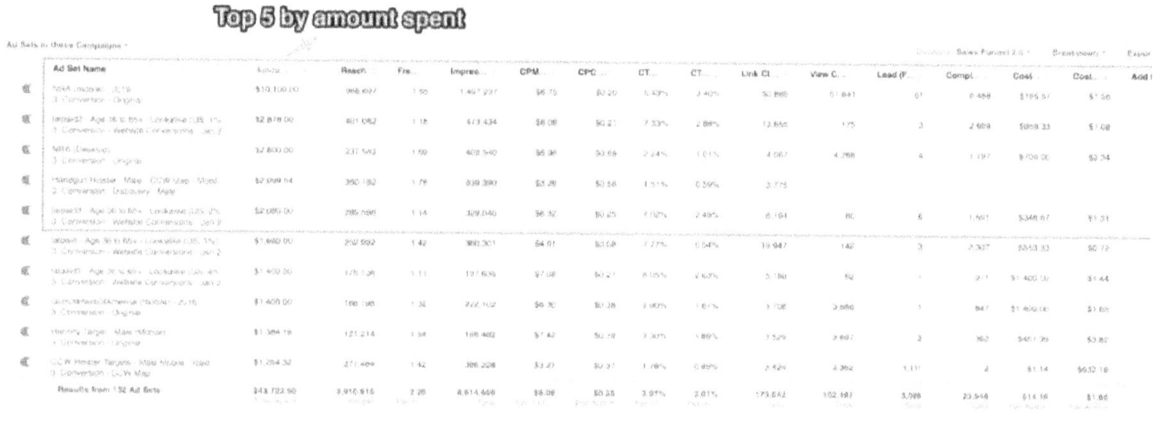

*Image 11.6: Campaigns by Stage Example*

## Step 2.

Check for Plumbing (For example, tracking errors) and Amplification (For example, audience or ads placed in the wrong campaign) problems.

*Image 11.7: Example of Tracking Problem*

## Step 3.

- Start with the most important metrics:
  - Audience Campaigns: Fan count and CPF.
  - Consideration Campaigns: RCS (reactions, comments, and shares) and CPE.
  - Conversion Campaigns: Lead/Sale count and CPL/CPA.
- Highlight ad sets with metrics above target. For example, CPL = $2.34 is higher than the breakeven target of $1.80.
- Break down metrics to find out the true cause. For example, CPL can be broken into CPC/CR. Is CPC too high or conversion rates too low? Make appropriate recommendations.

- Next, highlight ad sets with suspicious-looking metrics. For example, CPL is 10% of what the other ad sets have.
- Check for tracking errors. For example, pixel firing multiple times on the thank you page.

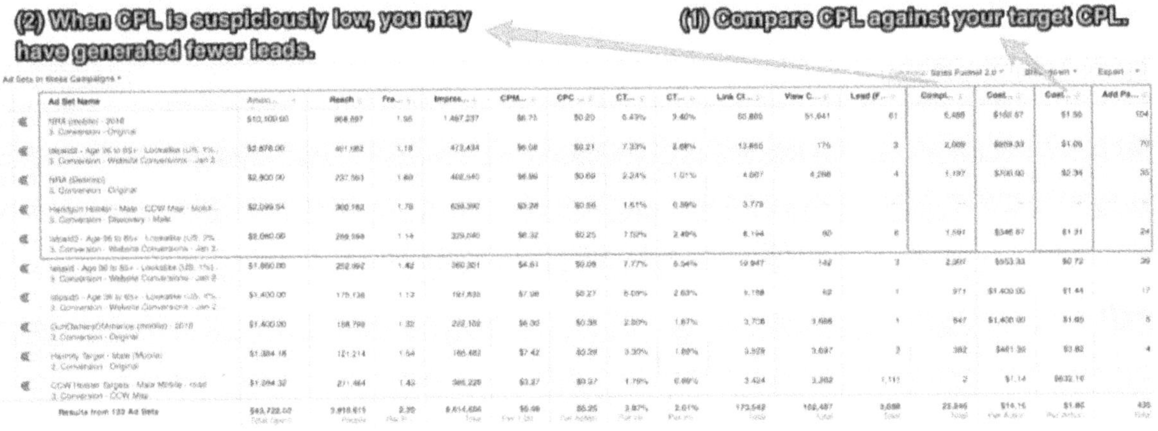

*Image 11.8: Example of Metric Issues*

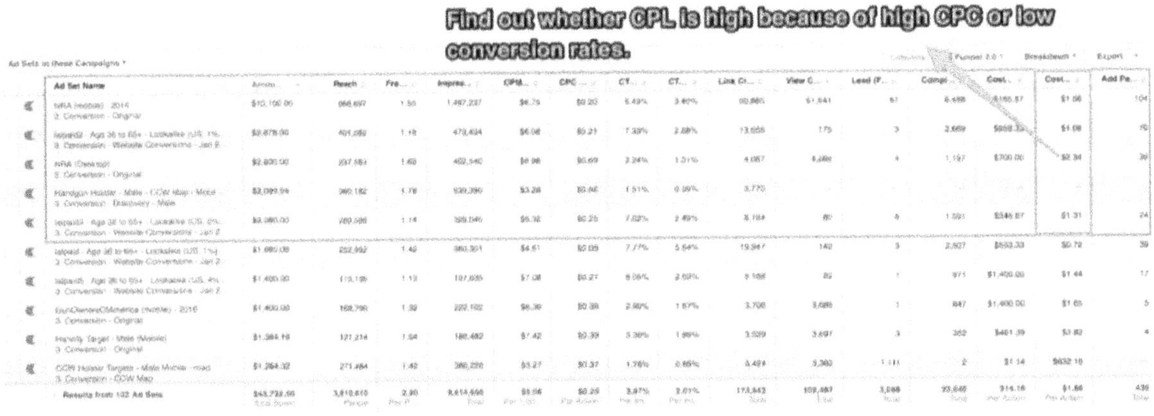

*Image 11.9: CPL Diagnostics Example*

## Step 4.
Tabulate the metrics, analysis, and actions.

| METRICS | ANALYSIS | ACTION |
|---|---|---|
| No results on TikTok events for a particular ad set. | Tracking is probably broken on the site. | Check if TikTok pixels are firing on the landing page (pageview) and the thank you page (pageview, lead/registration). |
| Your Desktop's | Conversion rates are | Tweak ads in the Desktop, |

| | | |
|---|---|---|
| CPL is higher than targeted. | consistent with other ad sets. However, CTR (link) is significantly lower than the rest of the top 5 (e.g. 1.01% vs 2.88% for lalpaid2). | Analyze the ads inside the ad set separately. |
| Mobile has the highest CTR (link) of 3.40% among the top 5 ads but has the second highest CPL. | Mobile has a lower conversion rate than lalpaid2 and lalpaid3:<br>• Mobile: 12.8%<br>• Lalpaid2: 19.5%<br>• Lalpaid3: 19.4% | Analyze ads inside Mobile. Mobile is using a lot more of SixThings ads, which has a higher CTR but lower conversion rate than the CCG ads. Implement and test CCG ads for ad sets. Obtain SIDs from the client. |
| Lalpaid2 and Lalpaid3's CPL are lower than the target CPL of $2. | Profit is not maximized. | Increase the daily budget for Lalpaid2 and Lalpaid3 until we maximize profit (i.e., maximize volume vs margin trade-off). |

## Step 5.

Next, sort ad sets by lead count.

## Repeat Steps 2-4.

When you sort by lead or conversion, this should only be applicable to your conversion campaign.

| Ad Set Name | Amount... | Reach | Fre... | Impres... | CPM... | CPC ... | CT... | CT... | Link Cl... | View C... | Lead (F... | Con... | Cost... | Cost... | Add |
|---|---|---|---|---|---|---|---|---|---|---|---|---|---|---|---|
| NRA (mobile) - 2016 / 3 Conversion - Original | $10,100.00 | 968,697 | 1.55 | 1,497,237 | $6.75 | $0.20 | 5.43% | 3.40% | 50,689 | 51,648 | 62 | 6,489 | $162.90 | $1.56 | |
| latpaid2 - Age 35 to 65+ - Lookalike (US, 1%) - 3 Conversion - Website Conversions - Jan 2 | $2,978.00 | 401,082 | 1.18 | 475,434 | $6.06 | $0.21 | 7.39% | 2.89% | 13,657 | 175 | 3 | 2,869 | $989.33 | $1.06 | |
| latpaid - Age 35 to 65+ - Lookalike (US, 1%) - 3 Conversion - Website Conversions - Jan 2 | $1,660.00 | 252,993 | 1.42 | 360,361 | $4.61 | $0.08 | 1.77% | 6.94% | 19,948 | 142 | 3 | 2,301 | $553.33 | $0.72 | |
| latpaid3 - Age 36 to 65+ - Lookalike (US, 2%) - 3 Conversion - Website Conversions - Jan 2 | $2,080.00 | 289,686 | 1.14 | 329,040 | $6.32 | $0.25 | 7.03% | 2.49% | 8,154 | 80 | 6 | 1,591 | $346.67 | $1.31 | |
| NRA (Desktop) - 3 Conversion - Original | $2,800.00 | 237,563 | 1.69 | 402,540 | $6.96 | $0.69 | 2.24% | 1.01% | 4,087 | 4,269 | 4 | 1,197 | $700.00 | $0.34 | |
| latpaid5 - Age 36 to 65+ - Lookalike (US, 4%) - 3 Conversion - Website Conversions - Jan 2 | $1,400.00 | 175,138 | 1.13 | 197,635 | $7.08 | $0.27 | 6.09% | 2.60% | 5,191 | 62 | 1 | 972 | $1,400.00 | $1.44 | |
| RNRA - Age 36 to 65+ - Low - Right to Keep - 3 Conversion - Website Conversions - Jan 2 | $1,260.00 | 249,215 | 1.30 | 323,842 | $3.89 | $0.29 | 4.37% | 1.36% | 4,396 | 4,235 | 4 | 906 | $315.00 | $1.39 | |
| GunOwnersOfAmerica (Mobile) - 2016 - 3 Conversion - Original | $1,400.00 | 188,798 | 1.32 | 232,102 | $6.00 | $0.38 | 2.00% | 1.67% | 3,707 | 3,688 | 1 | 847 | $1,400.00 | $1.65 | |
| latpaid4 - Age 36 to 65+ - Lookalike (US, 3%) - 3 Conversion - Website Conversions - Jan 4 | $960.00 | 139,100 | 1.10 | 152,523 | $6.43 | $0.36 | 7.70% | 2.48% | 3,786 | 27 | 1 | 724 | $960.00 | $1.35 | |
| NAGR Target - Male (Mobile) - 3 Conversion - Original | $996.00 | 197,759 | 1.40 | 276,622 | $3.61 | $0.23 | 2.36% | 1.57% | 4,346 | 4,176 | 6 | 712 | $166.33 | $1.40 | |
| Results from 139 Ad Sets | $43,723.55 | 3,910,519 | 2.20 | 8,614,696 | $6.05 | $0.25 | 3.87% | 3.01% | 173,542 | 102,487 | 5,088 | 23,548 | $14.19 | $1.86 | |

*Image 11.10: Top N by Conversion Campaign*

## Balancing Metrics Table

Balancing metrics makes sure your analysis is solid and we are drawing accurate conclusions to help improve your performance. When analyzing your performance, you should always consider balancing metrics for your KPIs. Each balance metric consists of one volume metric and one profitability metric.

Looking at these metrics in pairs is critical to keeping the data we see in context. If a business is generating 1000 purchases, but the cost it takes to generate one of those conversions is greater than the value of the purchase, then that ad is not scalable. On the flip side, a low cost per acquisition means very little if the ad is not driving sufficient conversion volume.

Some examples of common balancing metrics include:

| No. | Metric | Suggested Metric Pair | Remarks |
|---|---|---|---|
| 1 | Cost Per Action | Action Count | An action could be an impression, click, or a conversion. Pair the cost per action and action count to provide context on the scale of the ads and answer the following Question: "Will I get this cost per action when I scale?" |
| 2 | Click-Through | Downstream Conversion | A high click-through rate is a good thing only if the downstream |

| | Rate | Rate | conversion rate is not lower than the other campaigns. If downstream conversion rates are low, it could mean that the content on the landing page did not match the visitors' expectations or that you attracted the wrong people. |
|---|---|---|---|
| 3 | Cost Per Click | Cost Per Acquisition | Similar to the pair of click-through rate and downstream conversion rate, a low cost per click is only good if they lower the cost per acquisition.<br><br>A low cost per click is meaningless if no acquisitions result from the traffic. If the cost per acquisition is the same as before despite a relatively lower cost per click, consider why the downstream conversion rate is lower. |
| 4 | Average Position | Search Traffic | Applies only to Search Engine Marketing (SEM). A higher average position may be due to the relatively lower competitiveness of the keyword. You can verify by pairing the average position with search traffic. |
| 5 | Cost Per Conversion | Breakeven Cost Per Conversion | The cost of each conversion is arbitrary unless you give it meaning.<br><br>A cost per conversion of $10 may be profitable to a business selling a product for $15 but is unprofitable to a business selling a product for $5. The idea of the breakeven cost per conversion is to maximize the no. of |

| | | | conversions until the cost per conversion reaches breakeven. |
|---|---|---|---|

## If/Then Logic

| IF | Then | Explanation |
|---|---|---|
| Audience size < 10k | Look to raise the CPA target or lower the ROAS target. | If the audience size is so small, it's highly unlikely that we get cheap leads on a consistent basis. Thus, we can ask for more money if the client wants very specific targeting. |
| TikTok conversion tracking pixel is not on the thank-you page | Stop campaign. | Conversions can't be tracked accurately if the pixel isn't on the correct page. |
| | Install GTM and place the pixel. | Install the Google Tag Manager on the page and on the landing page (if it's not there). |
| Ad is unintentionally inactive | Change the creative and turn it back on. | If an ad gets blocked, we have to change the content and run it again. |
| CTR < 1% | Change the creative (image, headline, or text). | If the CTR < 1%, this means that the ad is probably not relevant to the target group. Though if the conversion rate is very high, we could let a campaign run despite a low CTR. |
| Frequency > 4 per week | Look at the last 7 days data, then sort by the | If the Frequency is > 4, it is possible that we are |

| | dates. If ROAS or CPA target deteriorates for at least 3 days consecutively, change the creative (image, headline, or text). | showing the same ads too often to the same person. See if the seemingly high frequency is affecting conversions. If it is, we should get some variety into your ads. |
|---|---|---|

And that's the #MAA Framework in a nutshell. If you go through all of those steps and review your ads often, you'll be able to find the ones that are working and amplify those further.

## PARETO SUMMARY

▷ Just like on Facebook, instead of trying to promote 50 random things in 50 random ways— keep honing the one thing that's performed the best.

▷ TikTok ads are driven by consistently sharing engaging content. You need a constant stream of content to target your audience and feed your TikTok ads.

▷ The best videos for TikTok are 15-23 seconds long and involve movement, recorded on your smartphone with clear headings, text, and call to action.

▷ Metrics Decomposition is what we use to help make sense of changes in results we're tracking.

# Chapter Twelve:
# WARNING: Ignore This Chapter at Your Extreme Peril

This chapter is critical to the longevity of your business. If you don't heed the advice in this chapter, rest assured you'll wake up one day to find your cash flow has stopped and your business is dead in the water.

You'll find yourself mortgaging your house to meet payroll and praying to the gods of TikTok to restore your good fortune.

You need to read this carefully and take it very seriously.

The book *The Bonanza King* is a thrilling account of pioneer John Mackay, who made more money in the California Gold Rush than anyone else. It regales you with tales of crazy boom-and-bust swings as settlers in the late 1800s won and lost fortunes in California and Nevada. While *many* people made *lots* of money in the gold rush (let there be no question about that… in fact, the gold rush largely financed the Northern states in the Civil war!) only a handful kept it or enjoyed enduring success.

All gold rushes are like this. The TikTok gold rush is no different. And make no mistake, it is a gold rush.

The early days of online advertising were gold rush days. Google started auctioning off the entire English language, and within 18 months or so, the entrepreneur community was onto it. Chris Carpenter wrote an ebook called "GoogleCash" which taught people how to find affiliate products they could sell on commission - products either delivered digitally or fulfilled by other shippers - bid on keywords, insert affiliate links in ads, and potentially reap profits.

If you tested 10 products and campaigns, one was bound to work, and affiliate marketing exploded across the internet. This was the first thing that really got Google ads into the mainstream. Then, as vendors of absolutely anything and everything started noticing that searches related to plumbers /

automotive parts / exercise videos / you name it triggered these little ads to show up, they got curious and realized they needed to get in the game.

That's how Google ads went from sideline curiosity to the lifeblood of internet commerce.

The affiliate commission model allowed instant partnerships to be formed and permitted advertisers to be 100% invisible to the end-user. You had no idea who wrote the ad, bought the click, and collected the money and as you might expect, it got dodgy - real fast.

I thought it was a cool idea… for testing ideas over a short period of time. But I knew it was a lousy business long term because anyone could easily knock you off; in fact software programs emerged that detected profitable campaigns and showed you how to rip them off for yourself.

Google's staff quickly came to *hate* affiliates - especially the shady 1%-5% who were generating 75% of the traffic - and who were often selling lousy products with clickbait ad copy and upsetting Google's users. This generated endless complaints about "ad spam."

One day, without warning, Google took decisive action.

Literally every advertiser on Google's platform who appeared to be an affiliate - or who appeared to *have ever been* an affiliate - woke up with their ad accounts frozen. Minimum bids for all keywords was $5 per click and Quality Scores were all set at "1."

So in other words, you could still log into your ad account, but for all practical purposes, you could do nothing and sell nothing. And all you got was robot replies to your emails and support tickets. Their staff would not help you.

I had one customer, Bill McClure, who sold coffee (not business opportunities, not horoscopes, not Nigerian email scams, not Viagra, not alternative medicine - COFFEE!!) whose account was "Google Slapped" because two years before, he had dabbled in affiliate marketing.

He did everything he could think of to reactivate or re-open his account, to no avail. He was locked out for over a year.

That's just one example. I had hundreds of clients like this.

About a week after that "Google Slap," I and my clients had figured out roughly what had happened so I hosted a teleseminar to explain what was going on. 3500 people attended that teleseminar. The carnage was everywhere.

That was 2005. This problem has been with us ever since. The problem is:

- A small percentage of users of *all* online platforms are always trying to "game the system" which creates a bad experience for users.

- It is not realistic or even possible for TikTok / Google / Facebook / Instagram / YouTube / Amazon to take a "laissez-faire" "100% freedom of speech" "libertarian" approach of "just let the marketplace sort itself out." If they did that, their platforms would be overrun with scammers and spammers.

- The bad apples are extremely resourceful and persistent.

- So the platforms try to police this as best they can

- These platforms use algorithms, low-wage, low-talent workers, and often vague guidelines to regulate the bad behavior

- They inevitably do a lousy job of figuring out who's good and who's bad. So they shoot a lot of "good guys" in the head.

In fact, all hot new platforms run through this cycle. I've seen this with Google, YouTube, Facebook, Amazon, Instagram… There's a wild west phase (which is where TikTok is now) and then there's a maturing phase where a LOT of players get weeded out. The same crackdowns Google started doing in 2005, Facebook started doing in 2013.

So there's that. But it gets worse.

Part of the weed-out process is escalating click prices. There's also government regulation.

When Barack Obama took office (favoring a bigger government than the previous administration), the US government tightened down on advertisers. The Federal Trade Commission started cracking down.

They pounced on Google first. They started fining Google for the sins of its advertisers. So then Google started tightening down too, *but Google would never really tell you what they wanted or what was allowed* since doing so would only tip off the scammers on how to evade detection.

So this puts a huge clamp on ads in every category that tends to attract problems: weight loss, health, fitness, finance, investing, business opportunities, and real estate.

But it gets worse. In 2019 Google banned IRS negotiation firms and alternative medicine from both organic and paid listings. Thousands of websites lost their ability to advertise entirely, and their first page listings moved to page 10 or 20 or else vanished outright.

This meant that relying on an online advertising platform was like dating a manic depressive and occasionally psychotic boyfriend. Some days bliss…. other days terror.

I've mostly talked about Google but I could just as well be talking about Facebook or TikTok or any of the others.

It's like raising kids with an alcoholic spouse who sometimes brings a paycheck and comes home for dinner, and sometimes disappears for weeks at a time. How do you run a stable business under such unpredictable conditions?

Pareto Point

The first thing you do is build an email list!

**Email is the #1 channel that no corporation "owns."** (Podcasting is another. Snail mail is another.) Any website can send and receive email without permission from anyone else. Yes, email is subject to spam blockers and the rest, but if you treat people well and don't abuse your list, the problems with email are manageable.

*The more the internet is driven by centralized corporations* (Apple, Facebook, TikTok, Google, Amazon), *the greater the asset value of your email list.* In the early days of paid search ads, I had many friends and clients making tens of thousands of dollars per month doing "arbitrage" -

buying traffic, sending it to affiliate offers, and pocketing the difference between the payout and the ad cost. It was the ultimate "invisible business."

It was tricky to make work, but some fraction of the time people would pull it off... then suddenly, without warning, a competitor would come in or Google would ban the ads and the advertiser would be left with zero assets. It was the internet equivalent of a shantytown that washes away in the mud during heavy rain.

On the other hand, affiliates who built email lists via that same traffic built a relationship with the list; they could live on back-end sales from that list and move on to new traffic sources.

### *You don't own anything on TikTok.*

*You don't "own" your followers or fans or likes on TikTok or YouTube or Twitter or Facebook or Instagram or any other social media platform. You are renting access to those people from the platform.*

### *"Your" followers are TikTok's assets.*
### *Not yours.*

Never, ever, ever, EVER forget that!

If you forget that... someday you WILL regret it.

Your mission, should you choose to accept it, is to take TikTok's assets (people) and make them YOUR asset that you own - your email list.

Pareto Point

The #1 purpose of any website is to get somebody's email address before they leave. (This is one of the reasons we don't advocate the "free traffic" model. TikTok stars and YouTube stars are extremely vulnerable to the whims of the platform.)

Your email list is one of the most valuable assets in marketing, and it really is an asset. It affects the value of your company. An email list is a resource that you can regularly go to for engagement and to make the cash register ring. **Email continues to be, by far, the most effective way to sell almost**

**anything - especially when your audience knows you, likes you, and trusts you.**

This means your #1 priority is list building. You should build an email list and a snail mail list. And while I'm not going to go into detail about snail mail, I'd just like to remind you that you can mail your customers a letter for only $1-2 each, including printing cost, and there has never been a time when people's snail mailboxes have been more empty. Contrast that with the torrent of content in all of their other inboxes.

Building a relationship with your audience via email is one of the most valuable skills on earth. The bonuses for this book include a "Look Over Perry's Shoulder" email course where for one hour I work live, without a net, writing emails for randomly chosen clients in front of a paying audience. **How Do You Wean Yourself Off Of 'THE ONE' Traffic Source?**

The fact that online platforms can shut you down at any time also means that you should <u>never</u> become heavily dependent on any one traffic source. And if you're completely reliant on one now, you need to fix that yesterday.

In chapter four I told you the story of the Wright Brothers and their hang glider and 12 horsepower engine. I explained how their low-risk prototyping method brought them success, and how likewise the "Unlimited Traffic Technique" says if you have the highest Value Per Visitor of anyone in your niche, you get to own the *entire* niche. I'm dead serious about this. Going from small potatoes to market domination can happen remarkably fast - and brings you diversification and security at the same time.

What works on TikTok won't usually work the same on YouTube or Facebook, *but it's not that far off.* Especially the offer or product itself and the primary reasons customers have for buying it. The holy grail in marketing is crafting an offer that works acceptably well across multiple platforms.

My client Teresa Sedmak founded Everbrite Coatings. They make coatings that preserve and restore metals for roofs, garage doors, jewelry, and industry. Teresa initially "pounded the slag off of her sales funnel" using

Google search ads. Once solid messaging and sales conversions were in place with good ROI, she was able to expand to Google organic SEO, Google Shopping, Facebook, Instagram, retail stores, and endorsements by architects and other professionals. Today she could lose any one of those channels and it wouldn't take her out.

Jeff Garnett founded Clean Slate Tattoo Removal in New York. He started with Google search ads and honed his sales funnels. Then he expanded into TikTok, Instagram, and Facebook. Once again, since Jeff has effective ad channels across multiple media, he is not a "stork standing on one leg" who can be taken out by the flip of a single switch. Oh, and by the way… after working with us for several years, his company got acquired for a significant amount of money by a larger firm, just a few months ago.

Client Gordon Gould's company, SmartyPants, sells gummy vitamins for children. He started selling on his website via Google, then expanded to Amazon which became a major outlet, then to retailers like Walgreens, supplementing their traffic with Instagram and Facebook.

Client Adam Smith was selling the majority of his moth control product on Amazon when legal and environmental pressure caused Amazon to shut down ALL products in that category across the board. This had a crippling effect on his business and he had to sell his car to stay afloat.

Adam's saving grace was that his product was outstanding and customers loved it, so when repeat buyers couldn't find it on Amazon, they searched for it and bought it on his Shopify site. He built organic search engine traffic with content marketing and relationships with pest control companies that resell his products. Three months later Amazon switched him back on, and going forward, he is not nearly as vulnerable as he was before.

The thread common to all these stories is that *they focused on ONE media until they got it dialed in. Then they pivoted into other media with a solid sales story and didn't rest on their laurels.*

Please don't learn this the hard way.

**Start with FAST Media**

The people in the above examples started with Google because customers are searching for those things on Google every day, week, month, and year. But doing your testing on TikTok (or Facebook or Instagram) has a different advantage: instantaneous feedback.

In a Google search campaign, it takes at least hours and often days or more to adequately test ads and accumulate enough impressions and clicks to determine whether ad "A" or "B" is better. But on social media platforms, you know within hours and sometimes within 15 minutes. This gives you many more test cycles and faster feedback.

These days most of my clients (including myself) start by testing on Facebook, then add Google later. As TikTok matures, we'll see more people starting on TikTok because of the extreme speed at which it sorts the winners from the losers.

**Easy ON = Easy OFF**
The upside of digital marketing is how fast you can switch on the traffic. The downside is how fast it can be switched off. Most people learn this the hard way. So (assuming you want a business with longevity, and not just a flash in the pan) you should look at high-speed media like TikTok *not as "forever" traffic sources, but as a high-speed testing ground for refining a message that you will spread everywhere once perfected.*

This is precisely how you go from "stork standing on one leg" with only one platform, to getting all the platforms you want.

**Ad Fatigue vs. Evergreen**
Ads on scrolling social media platforms like TikTok, Facebook, and Instagram "go stale" or "fatigue" within a few days or weeks. This is because the easily accessible audience saturates quickly. This forces you to constantly generate new ads. But that is not the only way to manage your campaign. Rather than buying as much traffic as possible, you can test an ad and once it's vetted, run it at a low budget like $10 per day. That may make it evergreen.

If you have 30 evergreen ads running at $10 per day, that's $300 a day or $10,000 per month of advertising that doesn't have to be re-created next month. That is a significant asset. I have many clients who have been doing that on Facebook for years. I myself have five-year-old ads that still pull in new customers from Facebook every single day!

## Feeding the TikTok Machine

In chapter 11, on optimization, we talked about the #MAA Framework—which is how to diagnose what's working, test and learn, then scale.

But most importantly, here on TikTok ads, it's simply feeding 15-second videos into the machine for $70 a campaign; testing in batches of a few videos per batch.

Then you can boost another account's post (Spark ads), which is the ultimate in "influencer marketing"—and no other platform truly understands this. The closest is Facebook with "branded content", but it's clunky.

Spark Ads is a tool provided by TikTok which enables brands to boost organic content in a users' feed by turning it into an ad—whether that comes from a creator's account or a brand's Business Account.

This powerful tool pulls in over three times as many likes and view-through rates that are 240% greater than other ads.

- 240% more engagement (boosted posts)
- 46% cost per action reduction

You can learn more about Spark Ads here: https://tinyurl.com/sparkads and back in chapter 10.

The big picture is that people are tired of ads—they rely on what their friends say. So we let the algorithm do the work for us by sharing what people are saying about us with the right people.

---

## PARETO SUMMARY
---

▷ Email is the #1 channel that no corporation "owns." (Podcasting is another. Snail mail is another.)

▷ The #1 purpose of any website is to get somebody's email address before they leave.

▷ Focus on ONE media until you get it dialed in. Then you can pivot into other media with a solid sales story, and don't rest on your laurels.

▷ The big picture is that people are tired of ads—they rely on what their friends say. So we let the algorithm do the work for us by sharing what people are saying about us with the right people.

# Chapter Thirteen:
# Finally Achieving Success With TikTok Ads

## Tales of Three "Impossible" Businesses

**Impossible Success Story #1:** Sunny Hills created a business I would never have imagined would *exist*, let alone be a horse worth betting on. It was called "Sunny Thoughts." Being the somewhat cynical marketer-engineer that I am, I thought his idea was too "froofy" (I made that word up just now).

Sunny was and is a passionate connoisseur of personal development. His project originally started as a set of seven audio CDs delivering personal, positive thinking affirmations:

1. Sunny Thoughts™ "I'm A High Achiever"
2. Sunny Thoughts™ "I Believe In Myself
3. Sunny Thoughts™ "I Love Feeling Positive"
4. Sunny Thoughts™ "I Love To Learn"
5. Sunny Thoughts™ "I Have A Burning Desire For Success"
6. Sunny Thoughts™ "I'm Independently Wealthy"
7. Sunny Thoughts™ "Action Is My Key To Success"

He set up a website selling audio programs. The end goal was to sell recordings, but Sunny's main objective was to collect email addresses so he could send an email to people with a positive affirmation every single day.

He set up paid ads, driving traffic to his optin page, where he collected email addresses. Then he built out his daily email autoresponder with several months of material so that each new subscriber would get the automated sequence.

He also put Google ads on his opt-in page to earn revenue by tempting people to click on the ads before leaving his page without opting in.

His thinking was: "If they aren't going to opt-in, at least they can pay me before they leave my page."

Sunny is also a Certified Professional Co-Active Coach (CPCC), and his most famous former coaching client was his friend, Hollywood actor Chris Pratt.

After Chris completed 105 days of the daily sequence of positive thoughts, he sent Sunny a thank you note to report that it had stimulated his creativity and comedy writing.

Sunny received hundreds of thank you notes from people worldwide telling him how his Sunny Thoughts™ had improved their lives.

**Two things surprised me**:

1) The amount of traffic he could get for this was ridiculous. He quickly built his email list to more than 170,000 people in nearly 200 countries. Apparently, there are a lot of people out there who like positive thinking and affirmations.

2) He bought clicks for a penny and made seven cents for every penny he spent on ads driving traffic to his site - not including the revenue from his paid audio programs! Google was paying him to build his email list.

Sunny figured out how to make water flow uphill - to achieve the seemingly impossible via ad arbitrage.

Some people achieve goals like this by being too clever for their own good, or smarmy, or by making ad farms. But Sunny achieved this through sheer force of will, simply because he wanted to give the world his affirmations.

When Sunny was 12, he was hit by a car going 75 mph while riding his bicycle. His body was thrown 33 feet in the air before landing on the pavement. After five months in the hospital, his physical and emotional scars left him with low self-esteem.

Sunny created his dream job because he was determined to inspire others. He did this while earning a comfortable income living in his beachfront condo in Hawaii!

It could be easy to wax cynical about what Sunny was doing if you only saw a description on paper. However, if you ever had contact with Sunny, you could tell he was as real and sincere as anyone you'd ever met.

I believe that what made him successful was 1) he was as diligent a student of online advertising as you've ever seen, and 2) his passion and inherent uniqueness were a force to be reckoned with.

I've seen many people bring their own unique brand of courage and resolve to marketing and achieve stellar resolve through force of will.

**Impossible Success Story #2:** The first time I met Megan Macedo, she was a very quiet redheaded webmaster-copywriter who attended a workshop as the guest of her client, Michael. I took little notice of her, but a couple of years later she purchased a hot seat at a "Perry Marshall Live" event in London.

She said, "I want to be the Brené Brown of Marketing."

"Explain what you mean by that," I said.

She said, "People don't have business problems. People with problems have businesses. I believe a business is the easiest doorway into the *real* issues in your life. I want to build a consulting practice that helps people solve their real problems, using business as a touchstone.

"Can I do that?" she asked.

"Yes you can," I replied. "You just have to understand you're selling broccoli and not cheesecake. It's not the easiest thing in the world… but it can be done."

She began refining her ideas. Her Big Victory came when she enlisted her husband John's talents as a filmmaker. She made a video called "Be Yourself" (www.meganmacedo.com/be-yourself) which encapsulates the essence of her work and story in 13 minutes. Suddenly people understood what she does - which before then had defied categorization. This was the impossible part - because sometimes what you do is so new that it's hard to explain.

At the end of the video, she said, "I'd like to invite you to participate in a conversation. This is not like most conversations you've been in before, because this needs to be more frank and real than most marketing conversations."

She built an email list. For the last seven years, she has owned a business that allows her to contribute what is uniquely hers, on her terms and not someone else's. She is now teaching courses, leading retreats, and mentoring a bevy of extremely interesting and unique clients, along with raising two young kids in London.

**Impossible Success Story #3:** You can't imagine how many salespeople come up with a cool strategy, announce they're going to re-invent the sales profession… and never get anywhere.

Ari Galper was a sales representative fielding questions on a conference call. The client expressed great enthusiasm for his offering, but at the end of the call, they pressed the wrong button on their phone.

They thought they had hung up but they hadn't. Then Ari heard the client say, "Keep using this guy to get a cheaper price from our current vendor."

Ari suddenly realized: *It's considered perfectly OK to lie about salespeople. Why? Because most people think the salespeople are lying to them. There is no authentic conversation.* Ari realized he needed to tear the entire sales process and its assumptions down to the engine blocks and start over.

He did that. "Unlock the Game" was the result. The premise of Unlock the Game is a core truth of sales that I've adopted for my own work:

*Get to the Truth, not the Sale.*

Ari has developed a cult following.

What all three of these people have in common is that they forced the world to bend to their will, rather than bending to its will. In so doing they all created utterly unique, personality-based offerings. All were assiduous students of marketing.

If you look at everything that works really well on TikTok, it follows this pattern. What this book adds to the mix is the direct marketing principle that it's far easier to build a business on paid media than free "virtual" media, thus giving you far more rolls of the dice with far less energy expended.

The other thing all three of these people have in common is a mastery of paid media. This is one of the most valuable skills in the world.

## Traffic Tigers Starve Last in the Jungle

Having taught Pay Per Click for two decades, I have always found this to be true.

I've got a long-time member Dan in the UK. Dan ran a successful e-commerce business. He bought paid traffic. He began expanding from country to country throughout Europe. He eventually opened a retail store.

But then he hit the skids. A bunch of stuff started sliding sideways (triggered by problems with the retail store, I recall) and he went bankrupt.

Then a divorce.

Funny how bankruptcy and divorce have this funny habit of traveling as a pair.

Dan hits bottom….

So he hangs out his shingle as a paid traffic consultant.

Dan discovers: There is ALWAYS demand for a guy who knows how to buy traffic. Always.

One of the reasons is that guys who hire traffic jockeys are already spending money NOW. It's WAY easier to get money from a person who's already spending it than to convince someone to spend it in the first place.

(Ever sat in a Denny's restaurant trying to convince somebody to let you build them a website? They say no and make you pick up the tab anyway despite having given them $10,000 of valuable advice they're never gonna use. Oh yeah, and then they gave $2000 to a well-endowed SmartPages rep the following week.)

Master the fundamentals of TikTok ads… and no matter what happens to your current business… no matter what happens to TikTok (!)... you will never go hungry.

## Successful TikTok Videos

Even though TikTok is a relatively new platform, it's here to stay. The platform has already become top in terms of internet attention and is likely just getting started.

The power of the platform's AI to deliver engaging content to the people who want it presents an opportunity for any business owner willing to step in front of a camera and create meaningful content. With an understanding of your target customer, a basic framework to plan and create content, and an iPhone, you have access to millions of potential customers for your business.

In this book, we've worked to show you how to lay a solid foundation for tracking your efforts. We've shared suggestions on how to identify your unique combination of goals, content, and targeting that forms your strategy. We've shared some basic strategies for how to put spend behind your content to amplify and optimize your results.

Ultimately we want you to be successful on TikTok. You are joining a new advertising platform and so the clicks and steps and tools will likely change. In fact, we've already highlighted some changes that are in the process of being rolled out to the platform. Despite all these changes, remember that the most important piece of TikTok or any social media platform is the content.

If you are willing to step in front of the camera and record meaningful short videos, you are halfway there. If you are then willing to test your videos with small budgets and adapt and change them, it's only a matter of time until you find the combination that works for you and your business.

We wish you the best of luck and we will see you on TikTok!

You can find examples of great TikToks in every business category you can imagine. Below we've selected a few for inspiration and to show you what's possible. Some of these meet the sweet spot of a great TikTok video length, 15-22 seconds. Others are a bit longer, but still have elements that are praiseworthy.

When you start to create your own TikToks, you'll be creating a mixture of short videos and some that are a little longer. The point is to create, not get hung up too much on exactly meeting the 15-22 second length every single time.

As you share more videos, your audience will tell you what they connect with most based on the view times you'll see on these videos.

### Business Coach
https://tinyurl.com/elitetiertt

Why it works:
- Creates something relatable
- Uses viral sounds

### Dentist
https://tinyurl.com/drkennywilstead

Why it works:
- Puts patients on video
- Uses a visual hook (teeth)
- Shows before and after

### Real Estate Agents

https://tinyurl.com/nicolebowdle

Why it works:
- Authentic
- Good lighting
- Evoking emotion (fear)

https://tinyurl.com/besquedahomes

Why it works:
- Creates a listicle (top five things)
- Uses artificial female voice
- Evokes emotion (fear)

### Real Estate Brokerage
https://tinyurl.com/vaynamaett

Why it works:
- Asks common questions people in the niche would ask

- Showing expertise and care for employees

## Mortgage Broker/Lender

https://tinyurl.com/themortgagementortt

Why it works:
- Authentic
- Listicle
- Humor

## Accounting

https://tinyurl.com/vanadertt

Why it works:
- Powerful hook
- Chooses a viral sound and turns it down to zero to hack the algorithm

## Chiropractor

https://tinyurl.com/occhiropractortt

Why it works:
- Hearing the cracking back
- Customer response, "that felt good!"
- Sharing the service

## Lawyers

https://tinyurl.com/ugolord

Why it works:
- Uses a popular commercial sound
- Fills the screen with the image
- High energy presentation
- Clear and concise

https://tinyurl.com/lawbymike

Why it works:
- Triggers a common question
- Incorporates movement

**Home Services**
https://tinyurl.com/home-services

Why it works:
- Immediately launches into a hook
- Shows the problem he's mentions

www.ingramcontent.com/pod-product-compliance
Lightning Source LLC
Chambersburg PA
CBHW080520030426
42337CB00023B/4578